Mondays in October

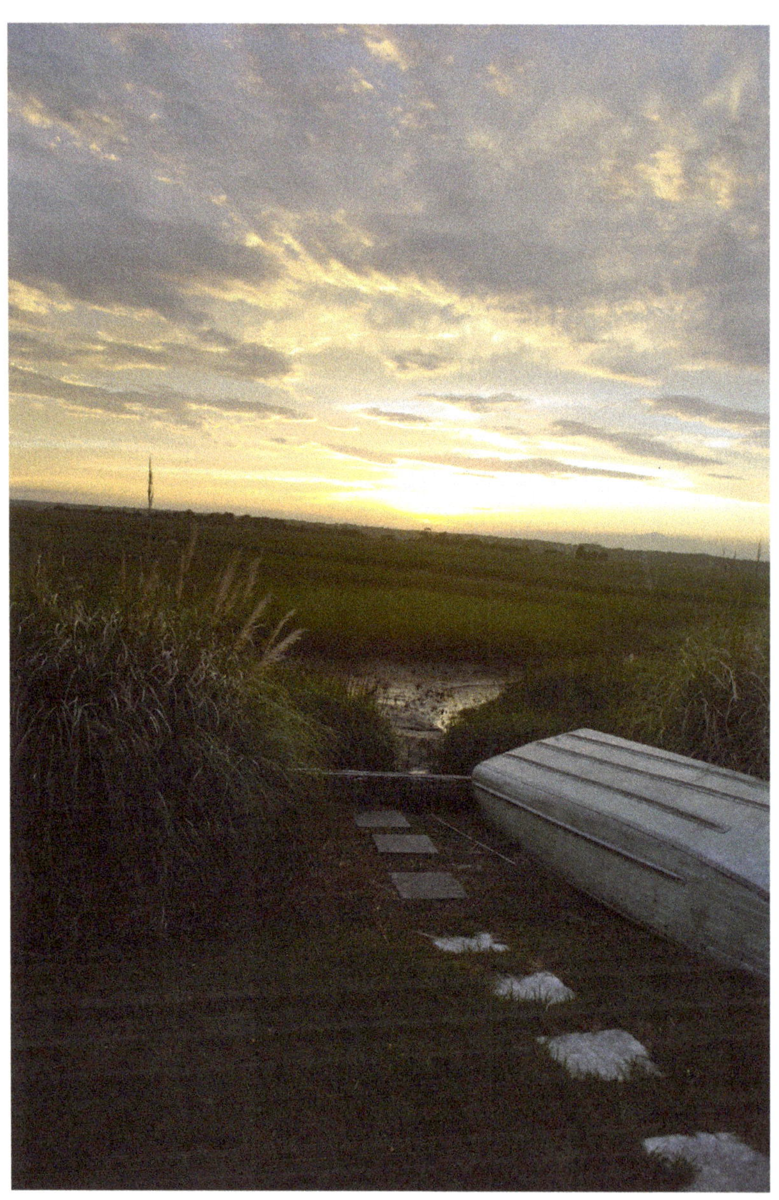

Mondays in October

poems and photographs by

Sheree K. Nielsen

Shanti Arts Publishing
Brunswick, Maine

Natalie,
Water is life.
Water is solitude.
Be Like water.
Sheree K.
Nielsen

Mondays in October

Published by Shanti Arts Publishing

All photographs, including cover, are by Sheree K. Nielsen, with the exception of *Encounter in the Abyss, My Sea Shell Life*, and *Sabrina,* which are by Russell Nielsen.

Cover image: *The Marsh at Sunset*, Sunset Beach, North Carolina

"Visual Perceptions" won Second Place for Best Poem from the Missouri Writers Guild Conference Contest 2019.

Interior and cover design by Shanti Arts Designs

Shanti Arts LLC
193 Hillside Road
Brunswick, Maine 04011
www.shantiarts.com

Printed in the United States of America

ISBN: 978-1-947067-44-8 (softcover)

Library of Congress Control Number: 2019936367

For all those who love water – in any shape or form

For Russell
These love songs are for you.

For my fur babies Sabrina, Bordeaux, Midnight,
Adeline, Elvis, and Ireland (Tater)
You bring me comfort and joy.

Elise and Marco
Your tango dancing on Sunset Beach against a
melon-hued sky is permanently etched in my mind.

The nurses at Siteman Cancer Center, St. Louis
Through my longest days of chemotherapy, your positive
attitude, smiles, and laughter remained infectious.

Remy
You made my day . . . on that Monday in October.

Contents

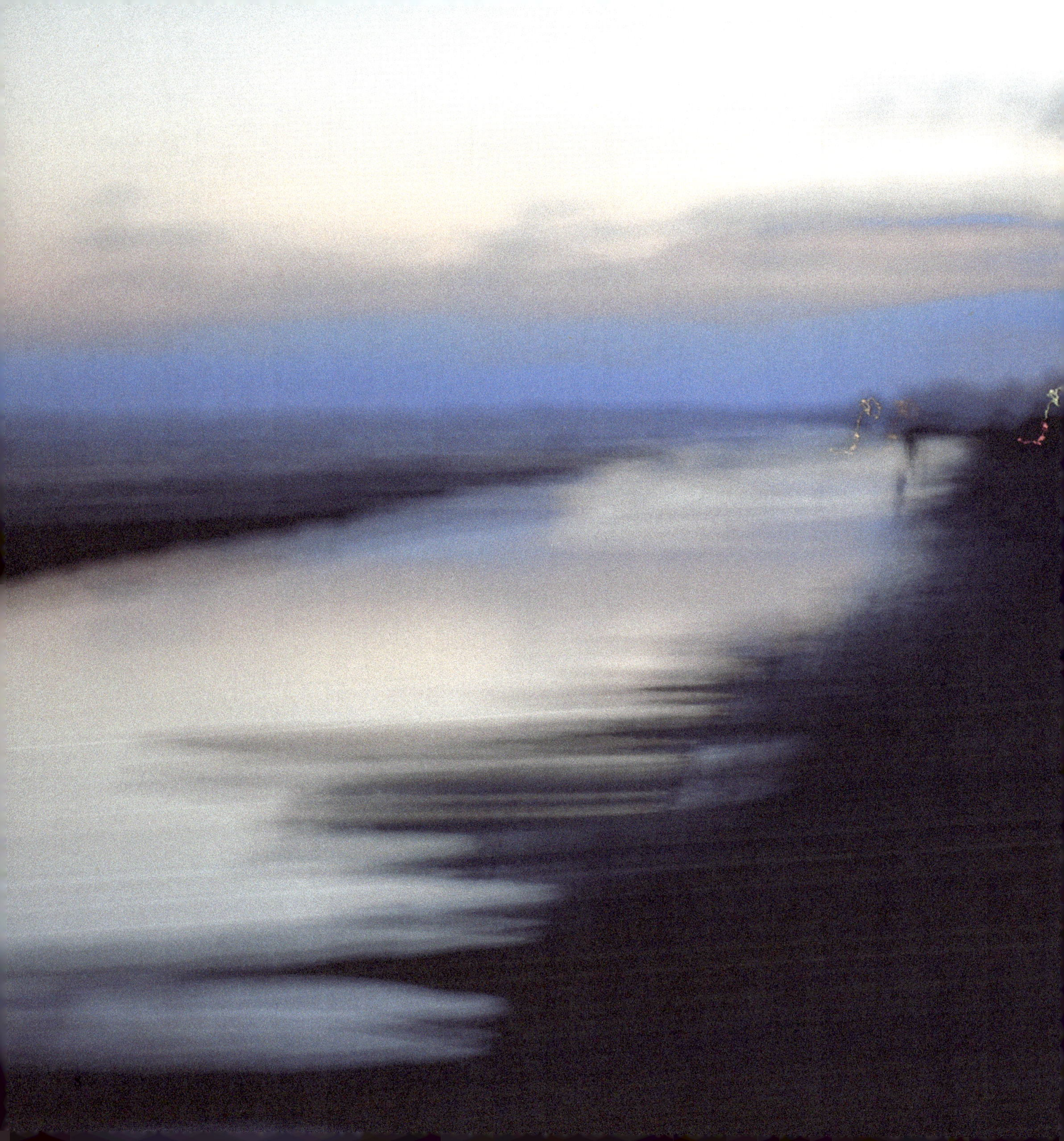

Beach Glass

At the beach, we become like pieces of smooth multi-colored glass, washing away our sharpness and softening us around the edges.

Section One

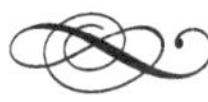

Song of the Sea

Waves peak and roll,
building
to a crescendo.

The wind directs
the ocean's
symphonic harmonies
with breaks
and ebbs.

Often
her cadence
appears deceptive
in the storm . . .

Always though,
serenading
the encore,
with gentle uprushes
lapping the shore.

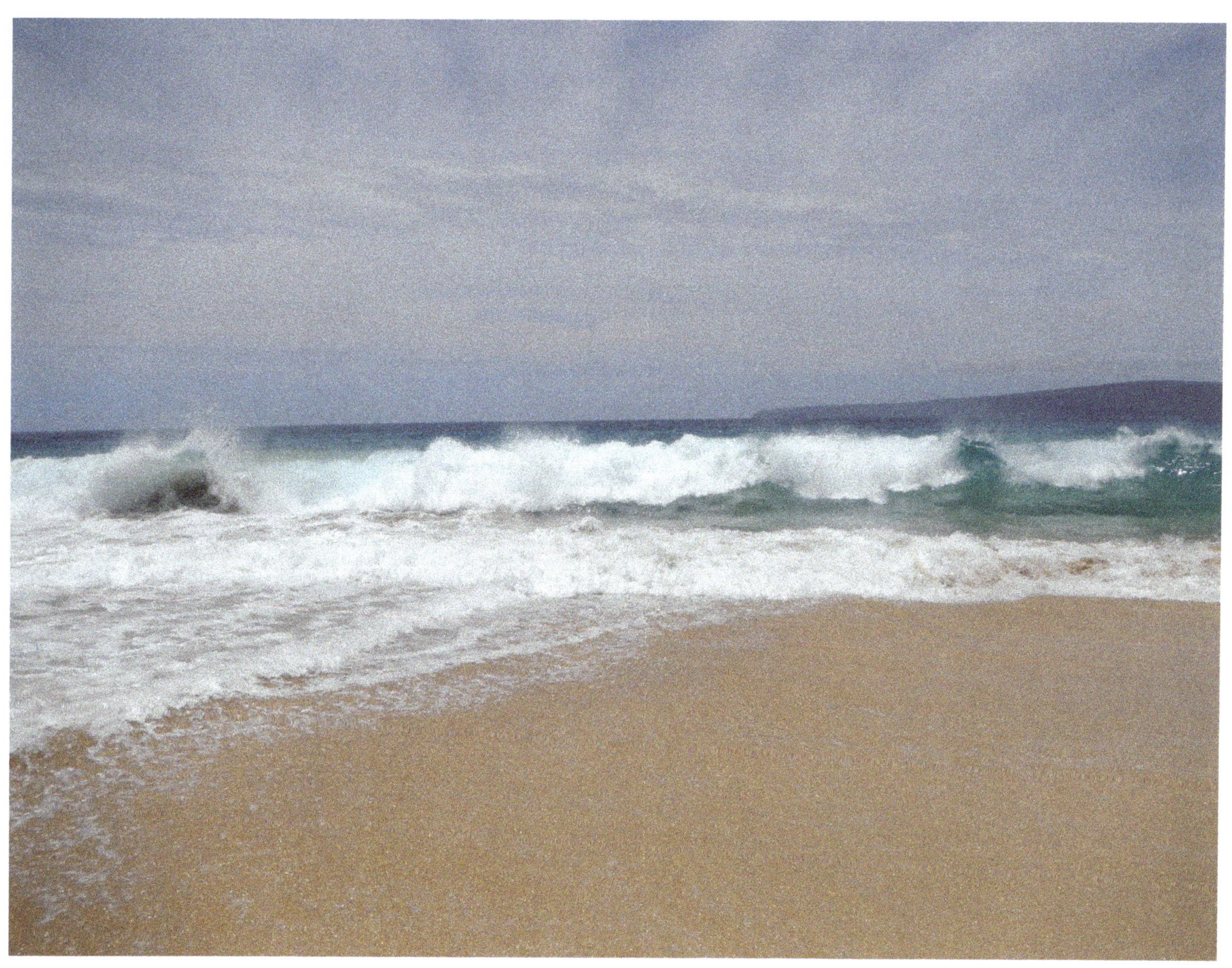

Haiku ❧

Out of the tempest
White boats sail where dolphins play –
a limpid lagoon.

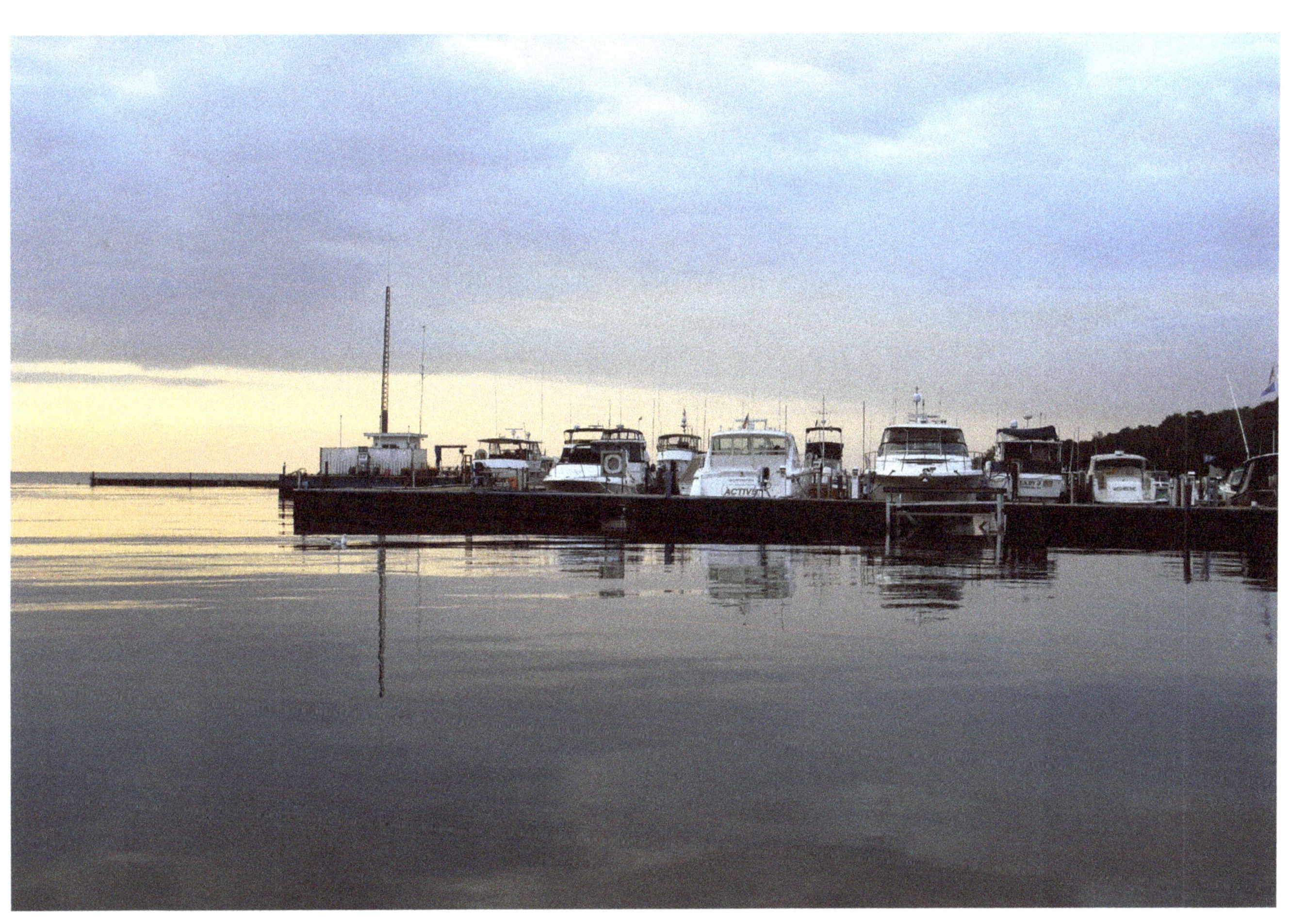
ACTIVE

Kite

A gust of air
lifts the ethereal
frame
of a bubblegum pink
biplane
sporting a curly
chartreuse tail
spiraling
skyward.

The sound of the
open ocean
whistles
with approval
and delight.

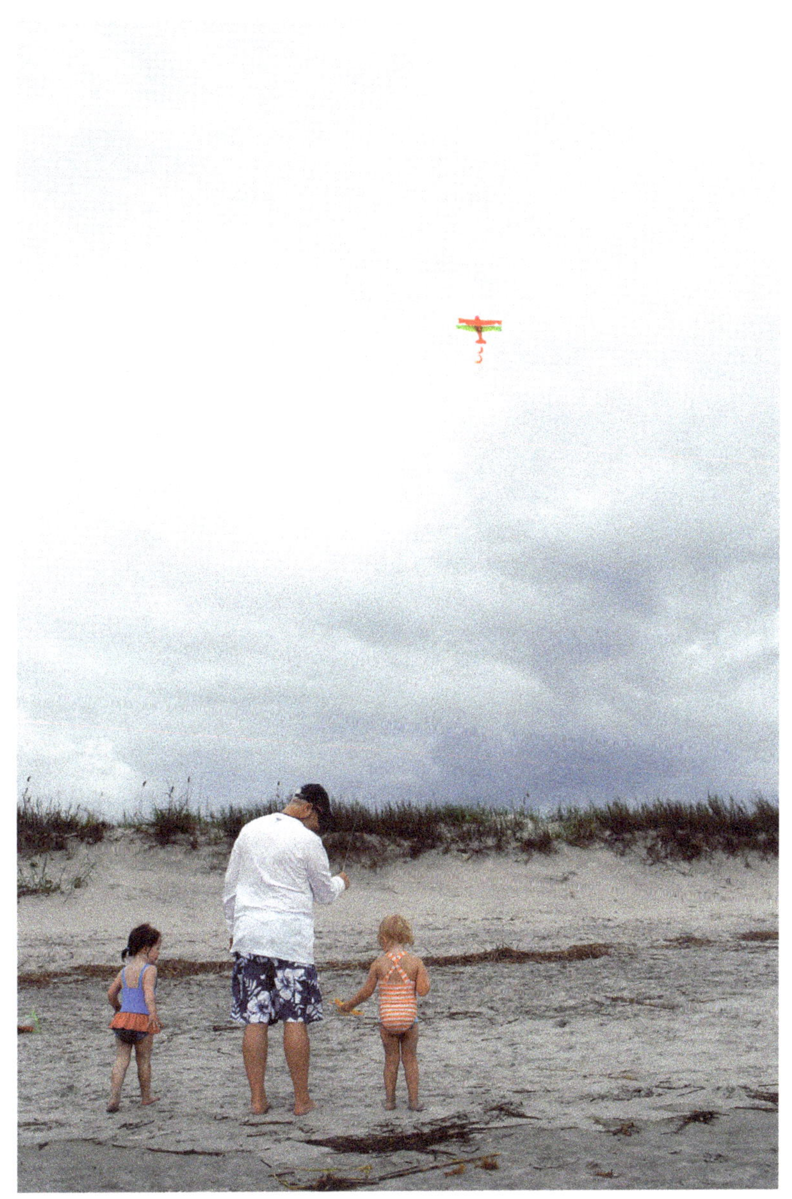

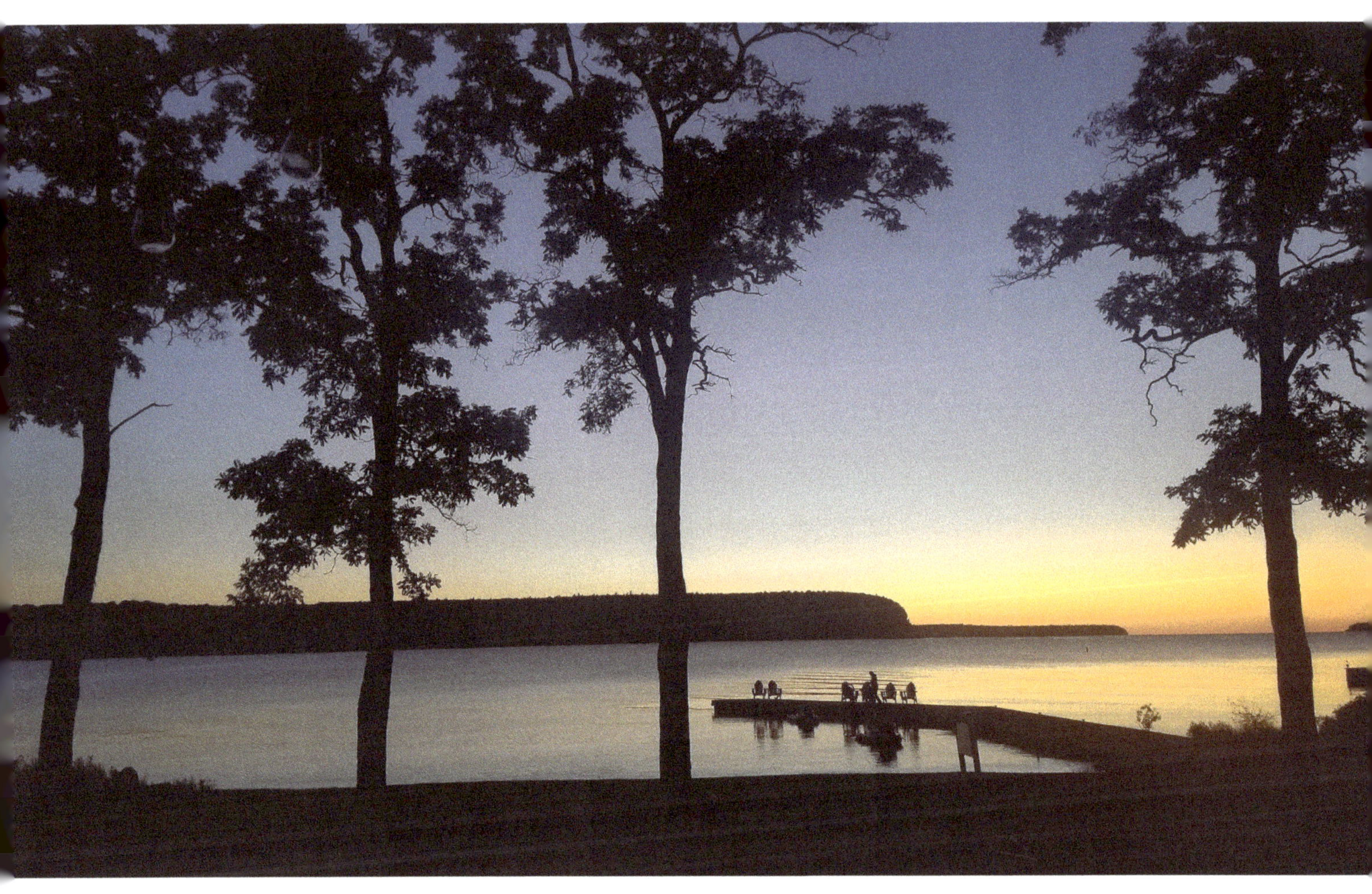

Waterview Blues

Bring me your
buttery caramels;
your deepest ebony, too,
and I'll paint you a
beautiful sunset
whenever you're feeling blue.

I'll throw in
a pink splash
for good measure,
a bit of cornflower hue . . .
You'll forget your troubles
are nye, my friend,
whenever you're feeling blue.

There'll be long docks,
and Adirondack chairs,
situated for the best view;
we'll raise some cherry wine
to all we've accomplished
whenever you're feeling blue.

Yes,
come with me down to the water,
where sandhill cranes
prance 'bout the shore,
and I'll tell tales
of seafaring lore,
whenever you're
feeling blue.

Whenever you're feeling
blue.

Whenever
you're
feeling
blue . . .

Dream Waltz

My heavy eyelids close.

I paint beautiful watercolor pictures
in my mind.

I dream of nubuck beiges,
washed out whites
and cottony blues;
colors representing
sea, sand, and sky.

Nearing journey's end,
my eyes
lift the final stroke of paint
from brush
to palette
to canvas.

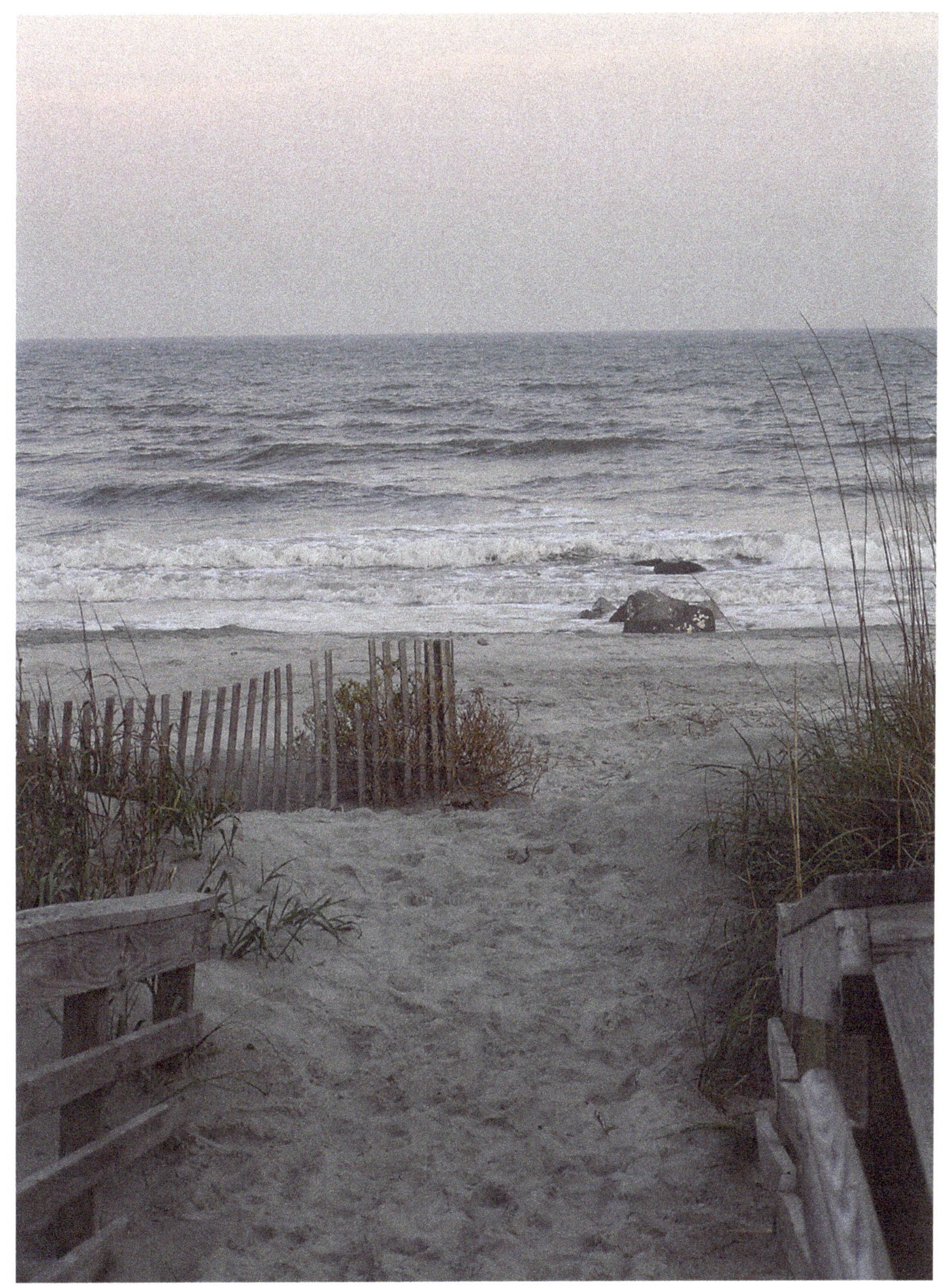

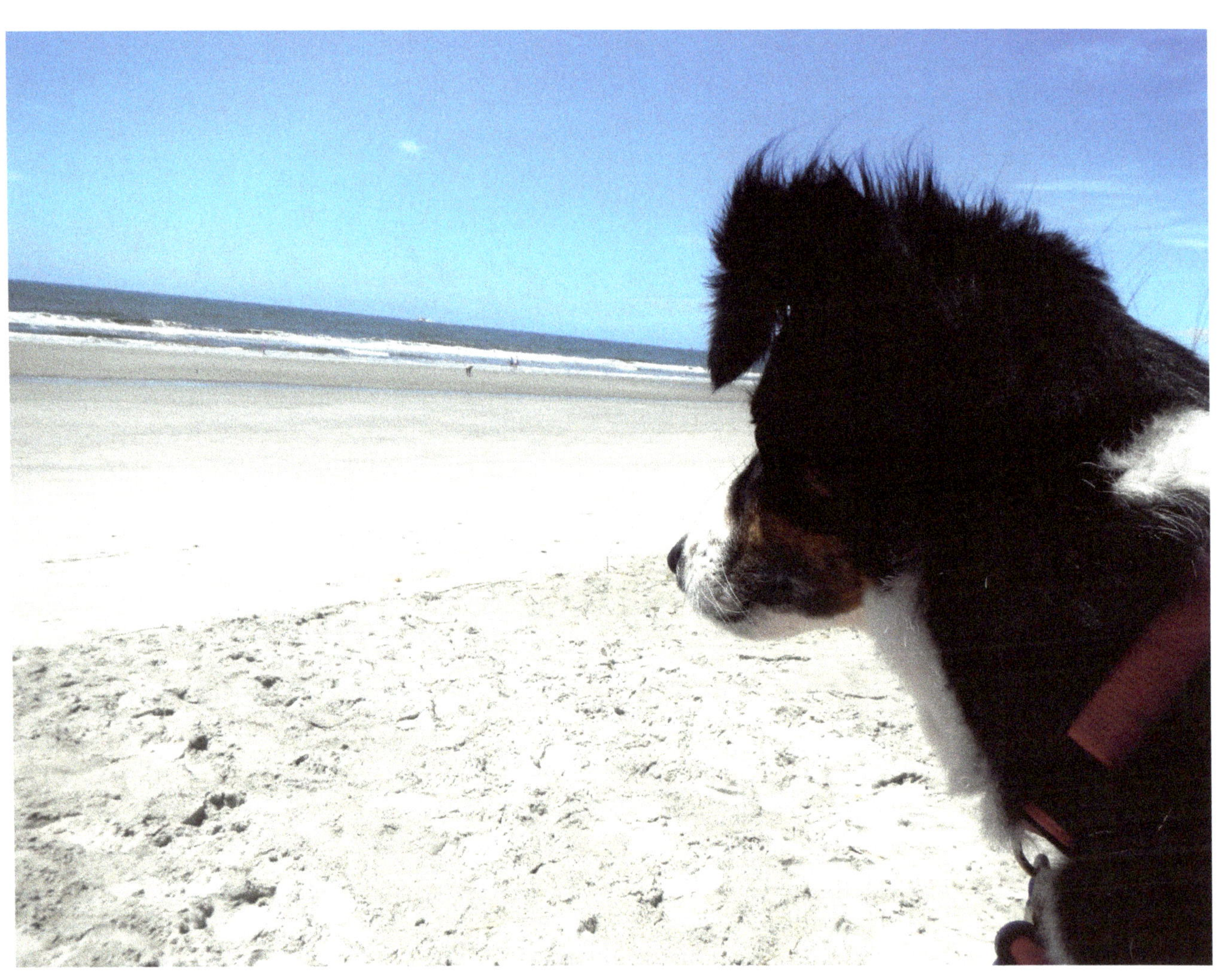

The Lure of Sunset Beach

Sensory overload
from fresh sea air
mixes
with the fragrant aroma
of magnolia,
and beckons those
who cross the road
and follow
a weathered grey boardwalk
to the shoreline.

My curious canine
with ice-blue eyes,
and lithe coby,
steps gingerly
in the sand.

The ocean
wraps its gentle
embrace 'round her.`

Wind blows
like a wispy seagull
tufting
lustrous,
coal black
fur.

Pausing,
she peers to the heavens,
and sniffs salty sea air.

The corners
of her flew
upturn in a grin.

Westward,
the two of us
race toward
the blood red
sun.

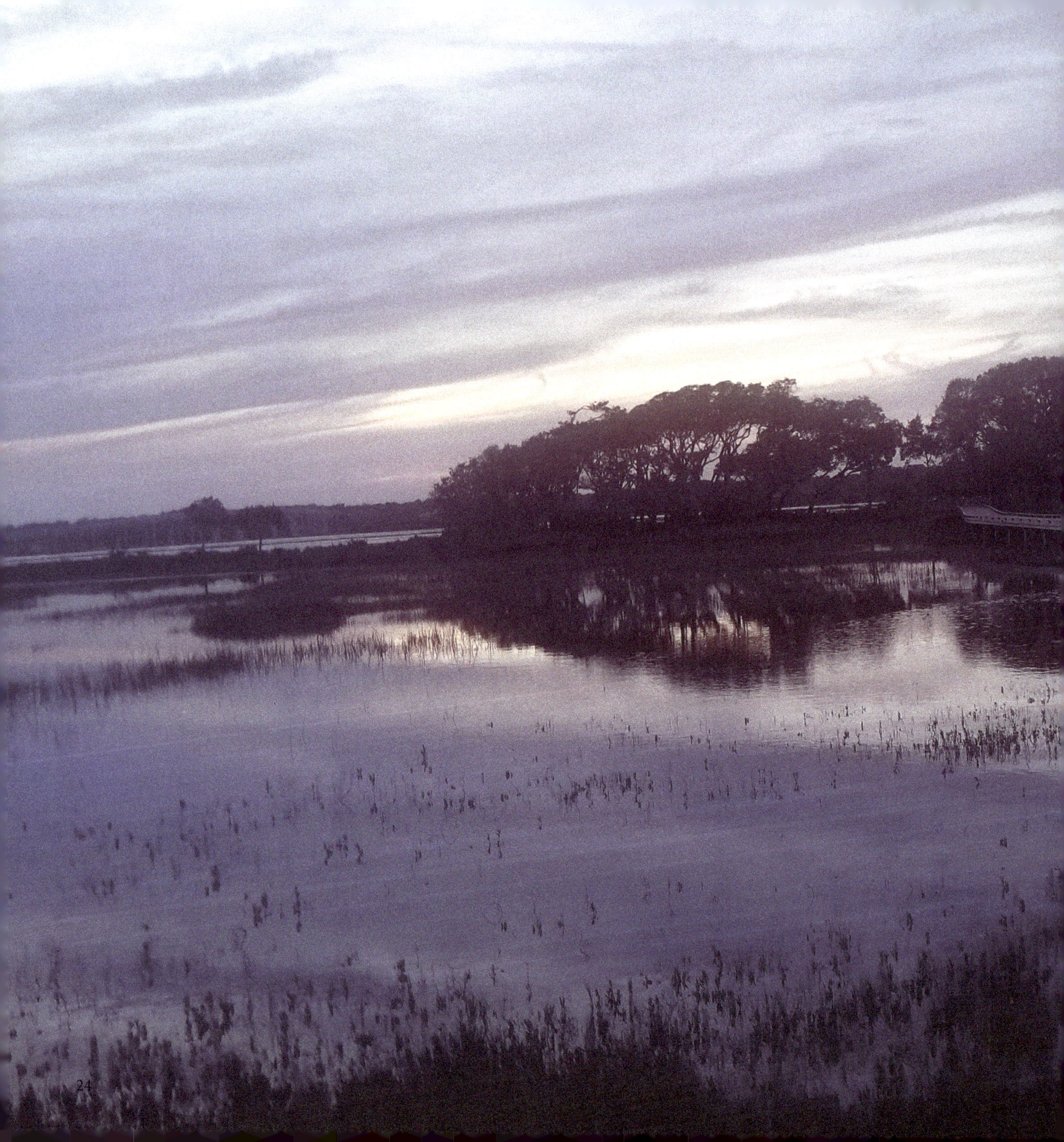

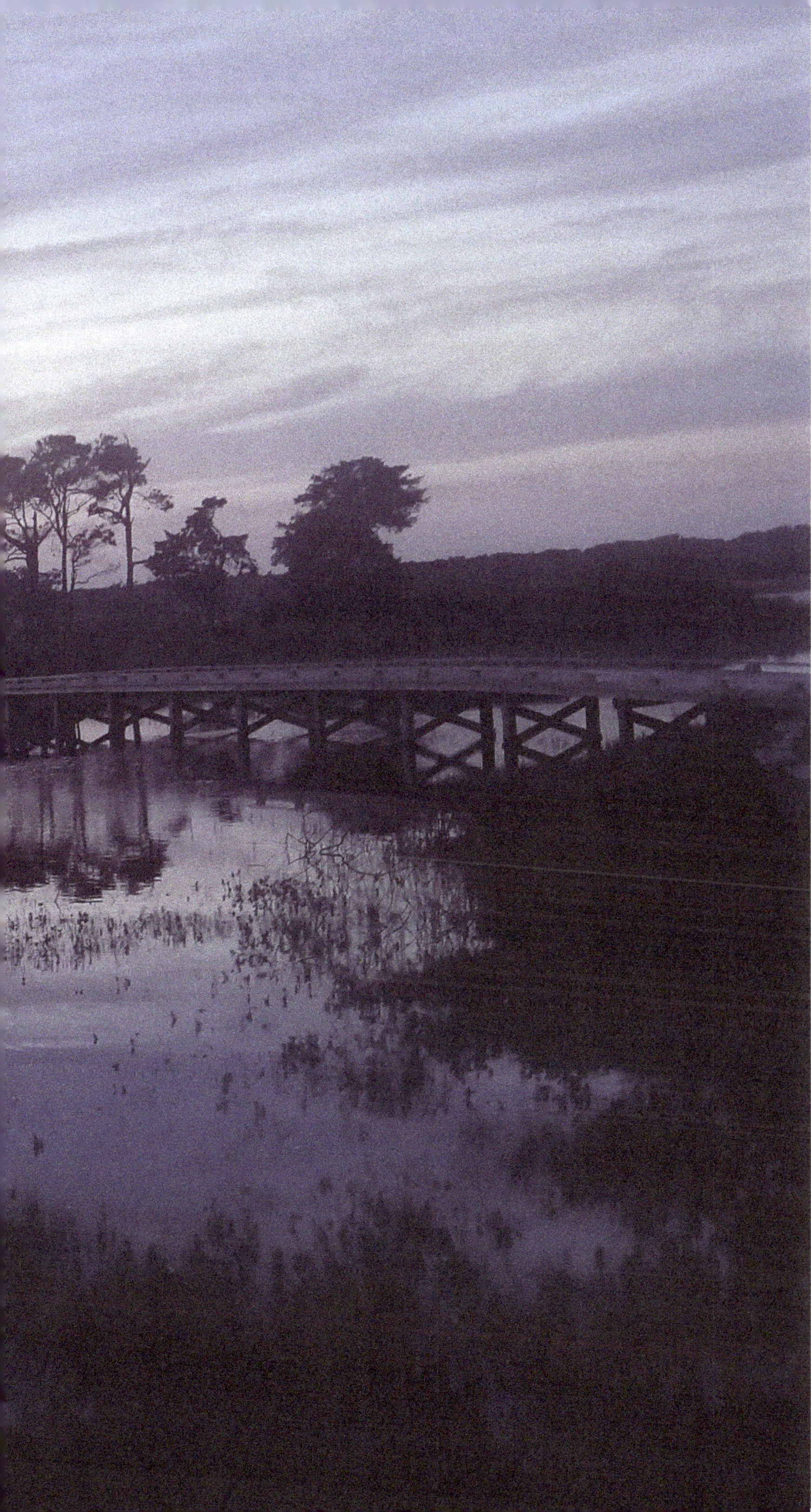

The Marsh at Sunset

The sky skips
daintily in
cotton candy pastels
and blue-violets
above the silhouetted bridge
framed by
ruffled reflections
cast on tepid
coastal waters.

Serenity settles in
as marsh grasses mellow.
A symphony of crickets and cicadas
chime in tune
to the chorus
of the southern leopard frog –
stealing hearts
and alluring dreamers
to linger
in her peaceful
effervescence.

The Kindred Spirit Mailbox

Come rest awhile
By the sea.

My pine foundation –
nestled between
an oasis of
salty sea oats
and
celestial sand dunes.

Impossibly
wide
beaches,
beryl blue
waters,
and onshore winds
await you.

Tucked inside
my malleable chasm –
a thousand voices
intertwined
in well-stacked
journals.

Stories of babies lost,
Lovers star-crossed.
Songs of triumph,
Songs of sorrow,
A study in nature,
A poem
to give
thanks . . .

Visitors
Seek comfort
And solitude
on my weathered
greige benches,
penning secrets,
prayers,
forgiveness,
on worn,
earthy
pages.

I am the fountainhead
to the outside world –
a lagniappe –
restoring hearts
through words,
images,
and universal beauty.

Those who seek me
remain
forever
changed.

Come rest
awhile
with me,
and I'll show you
the corridor
to my soul.

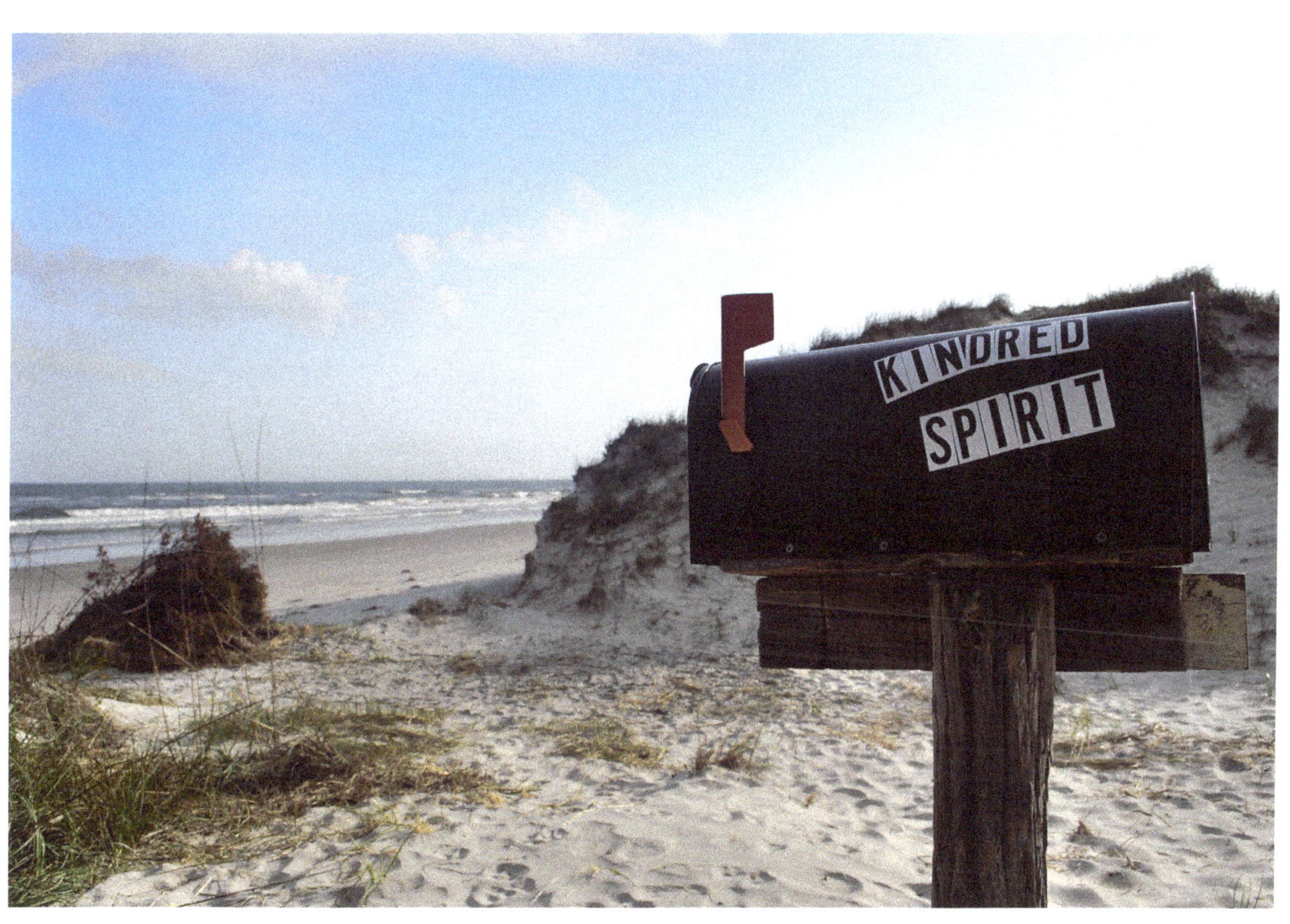
KINDRED
SPIRIT

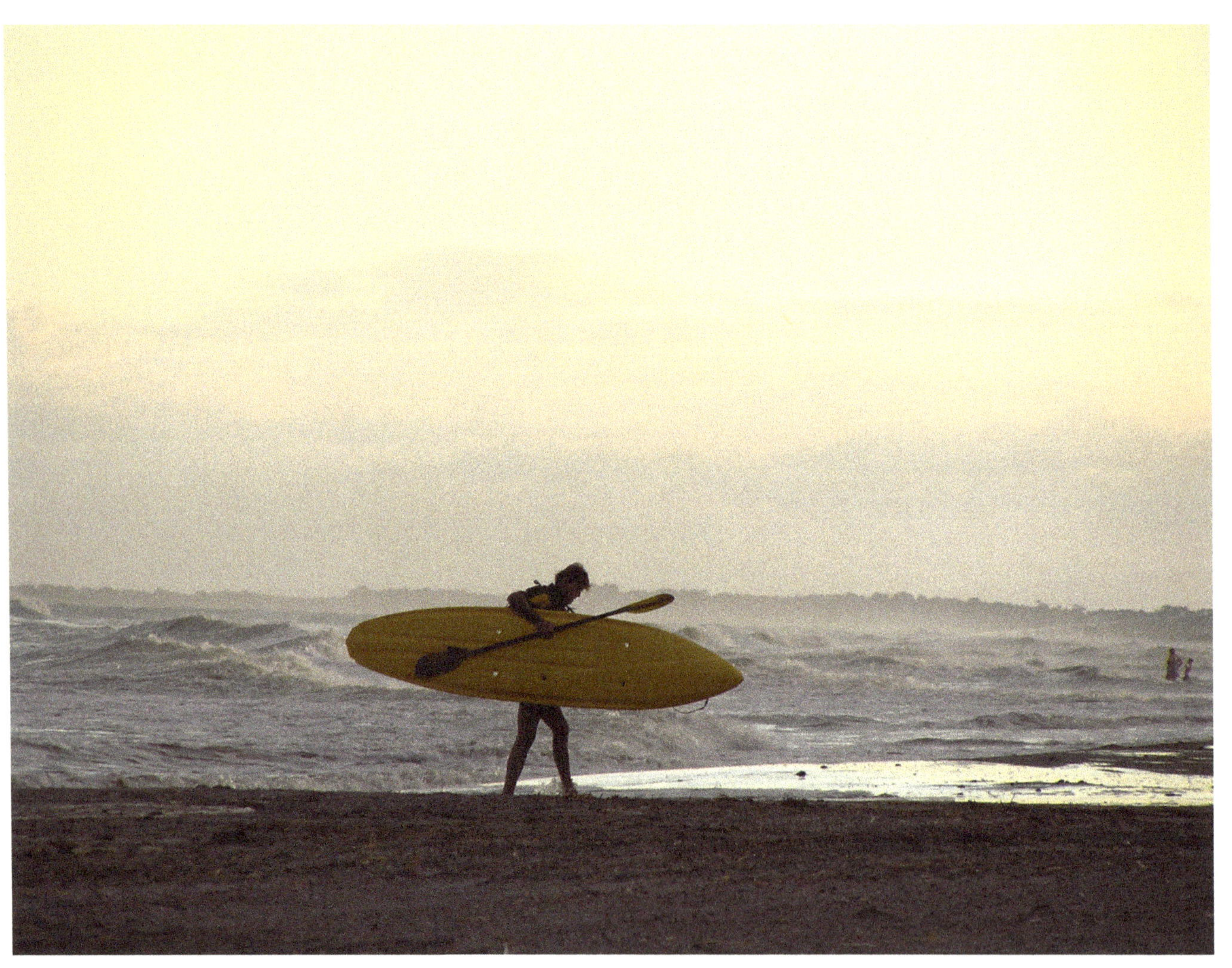

Living Water

Living water
rushes over me.
baptizes,
cleanses,
my soul.

Sandpipers frolic
in shallow tidepools
scattered along
the shoreline.

In the distance,
a white boat
skips and skims
the glassy sea.

Floating
on a pocket of air,
seagulls
dip and sway
searching for
sustenance
beneath
the briny abyss.

Driftwood,
once a palm tree,
blends with the island's landscape,
smoothed by the tides
and living water.

Crushed shells
mingle with sand,
massage
tired feet,
and wash away
woes.

Raspberry Point

At dusk,
I amble
a footpath
of mulch
and moist soil,
pungent
with humidity,
and the buzzing
cacophony
of
annoying
mosquitoes.

Lush,
citrine
Cinnamon and royal ferns,
low lying grasses,
and mosquitoes
brush
tender ankles
as I perambulate
the eerie
spruce bog.

Dark evergreens,
wild crimson raspberries
and fungi
abound
in this inexplicable
mystery.

I wait
for the
Creature
from the Black Lagoon,
but he
never
comes . . .

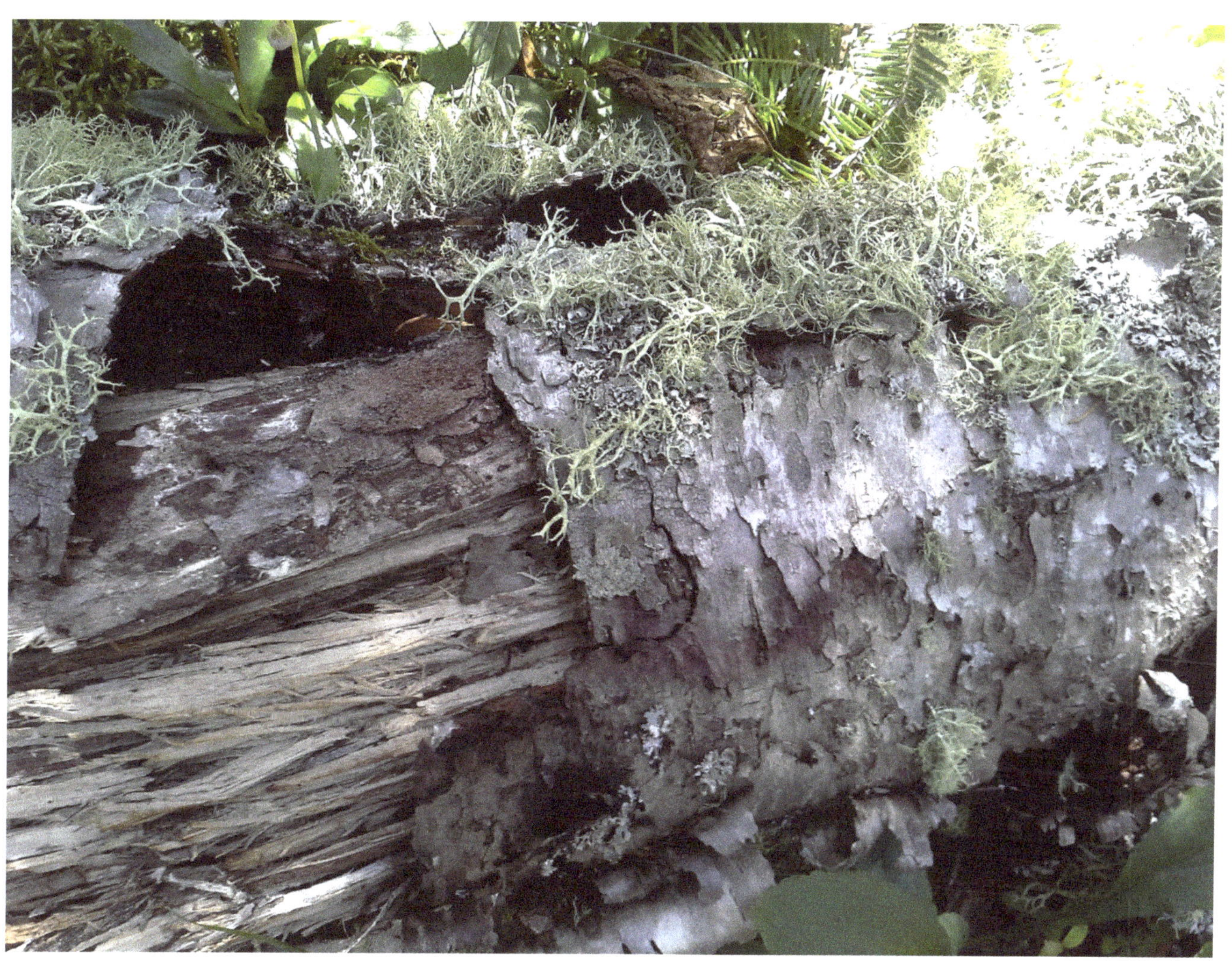

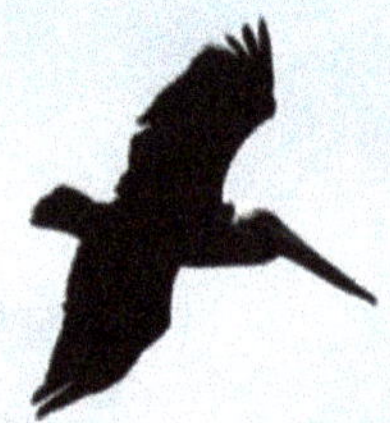

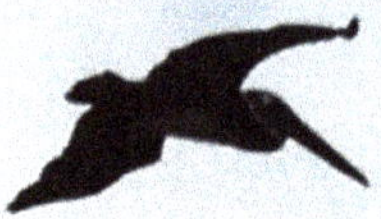

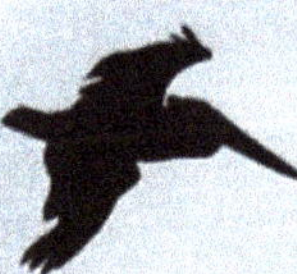

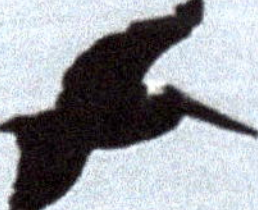

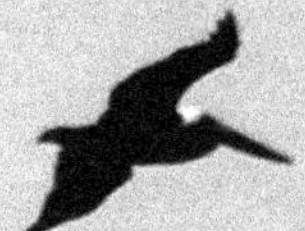

Summer's Kiss

Gazing skyward,
billowing kites
in the shape
of lobsters
and Labradors
paint
the heavens,
while
five brown
pelicans
soar
in F-15 formation
riding a gust
of wind
north
to
south.

Sea sprays
splash wet kisses
on my tawny,
copper cheeks
and wind-burned
lips.

Ode to Sunset Beach

I go down to the beach
to play
and cast my worries away.

I go down to the beach
to remember
a carefree childhood of yesterday.

I go down to the beach
to savor
glistening rays,
tempestuous waves,
and nature's folly.

I go down to the beach
to gaze
at lovers embracing,
six seagulls pacing,
and toddlers named Molly.

I go down to the beach
to pray
for sea turtle's gestation,
kindred spirits,
and Bird Island's preservation.

I go down to the beach today
because it moves me
with a wise silence,
and physical magnificence.

I go down to the beach
because I can.

I go down to the beach
because I am.

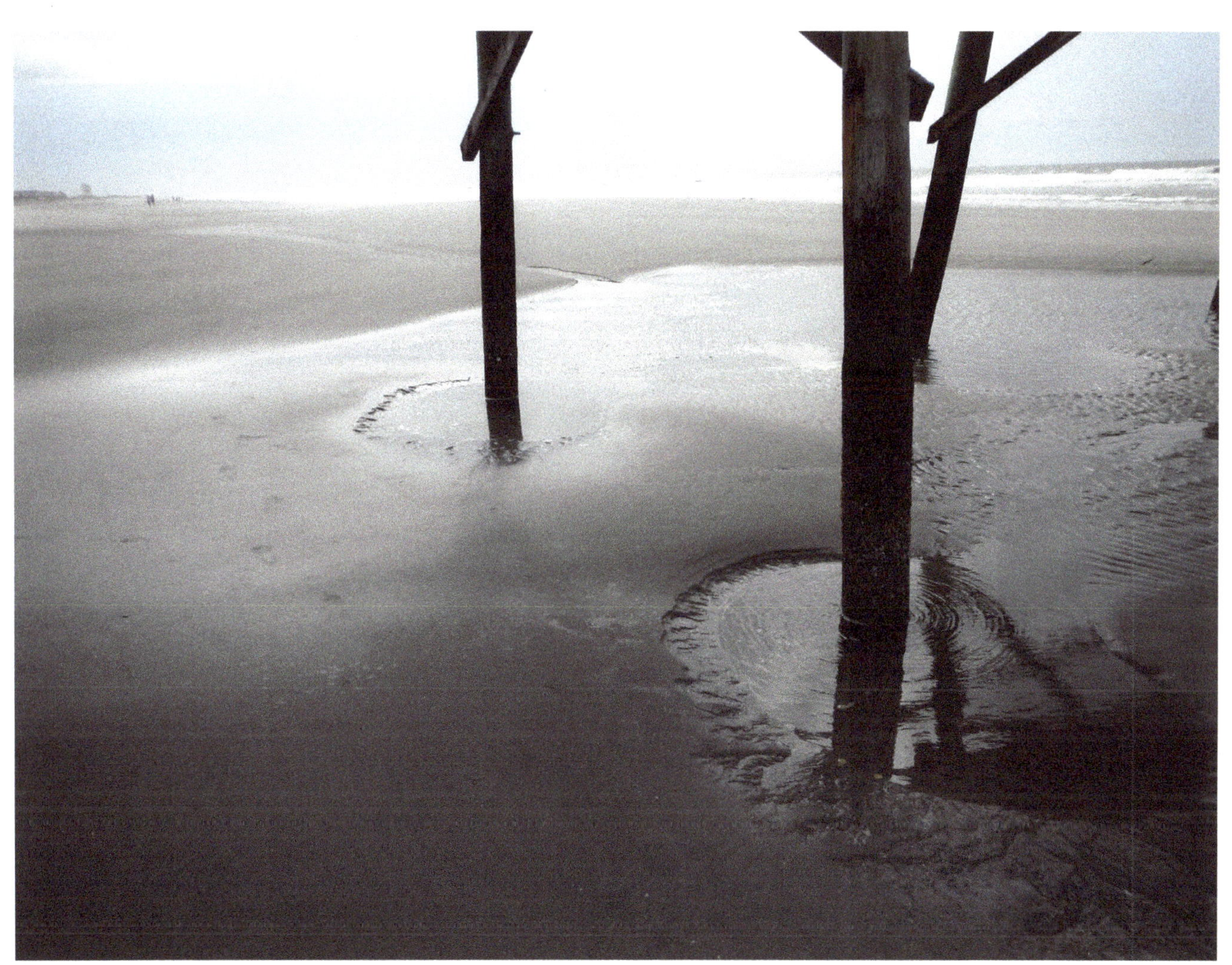

Section Two

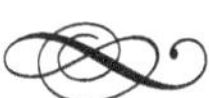

SHOREBIRDS

Six Lilliputian sandpipers
dip long,
spindly legs and toes
in shallow mud flats
watching
tourists
on the seashore.

Preening,
gleaning,
angelic wings
and brown-tufted
bellies,
resting idly
at ocean's door.

A gentle wave
pushes foamy surf
cradling
shorebirds
as they
prance about
lulled by
a subtle roar.

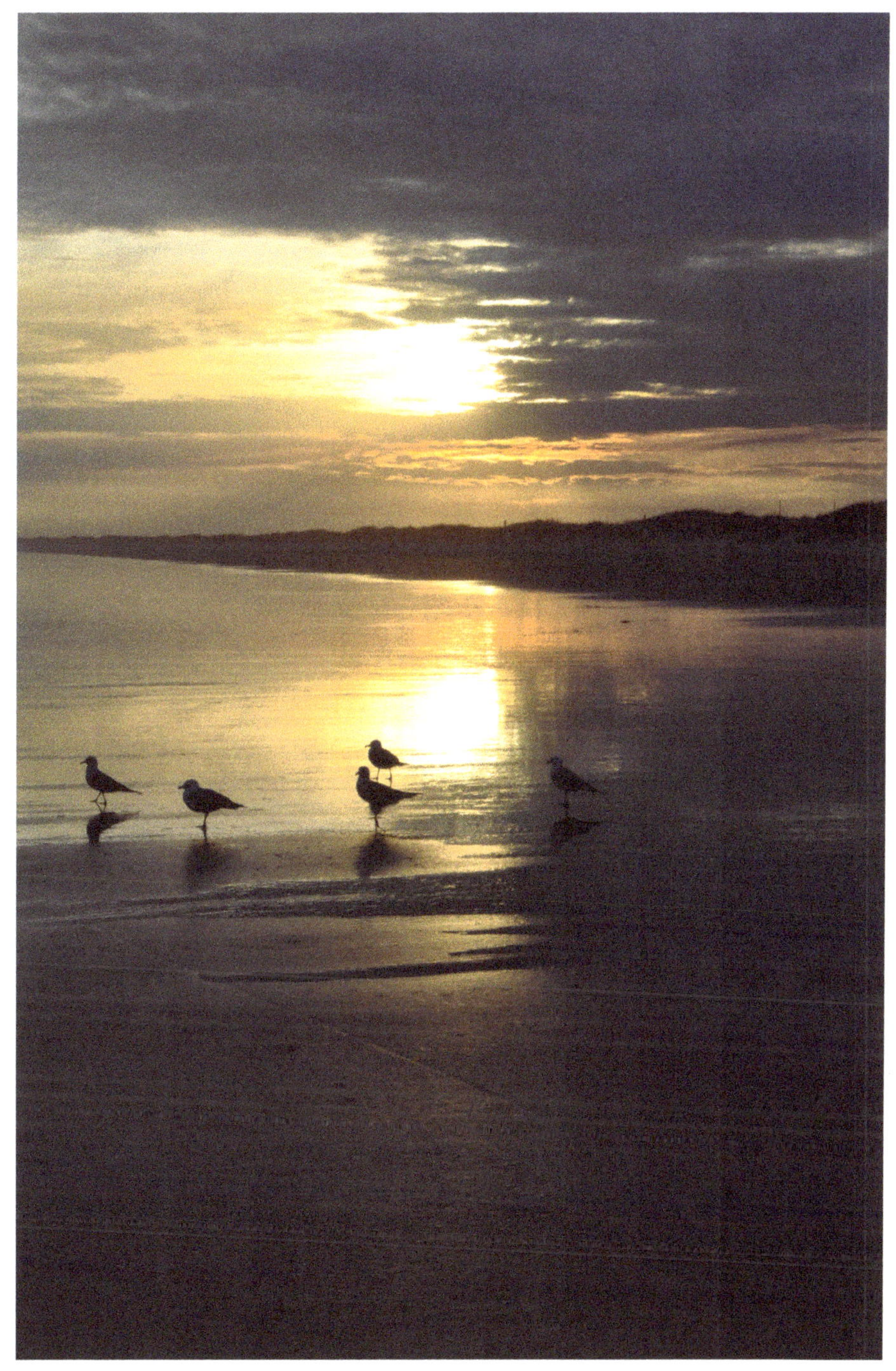

The Ballet

The sandpiper steps quickly and gingerly
so as not to wet his feet,
casually teasing the shoreline.
I smile,
laughing silently as I follow.

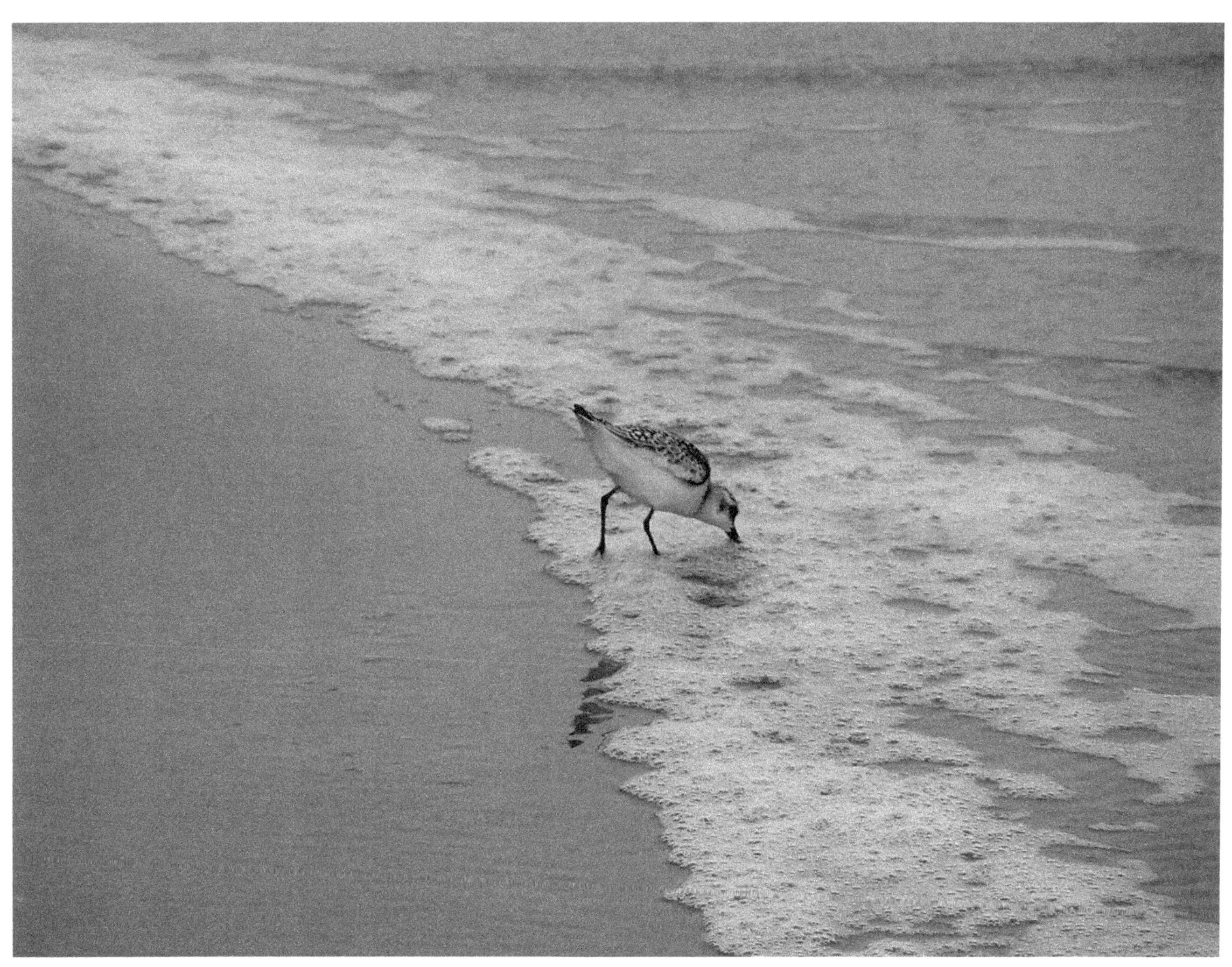

The Dancer

The atmosphere
morphs into pastel vermilion
and cornflower blue hues.

A delicate figure
of a woman
in sheer indigo blouse
and ruffled skirt
pauses in the shallows,
feet and calves neatly tucked under . . .

The tide lilts
silky fabric aside
exposing supple thighs
enough for a glimpse
of nectar.

Nimble fingers touch
liquid sand
writing messages . . .
only to be washed away.

Arising from the gentle embrace
of the ocean,
the woman dips and sways and skips –

Lean, sinewy limbs
glisten with wetness,
and painted toes
sketch
wedding band
designs
along the seashore.

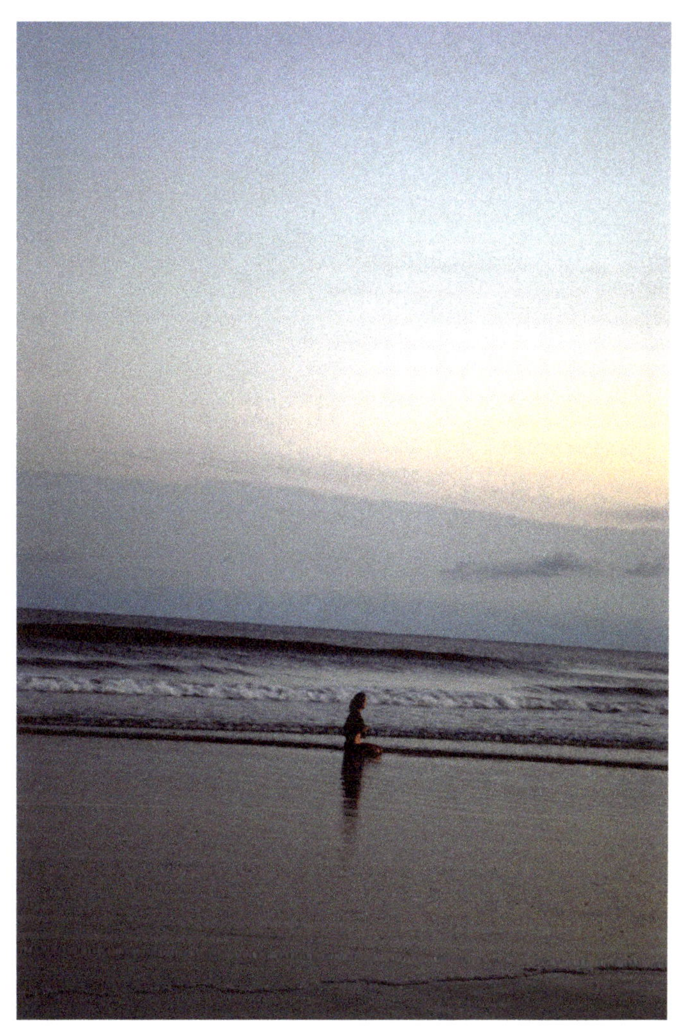

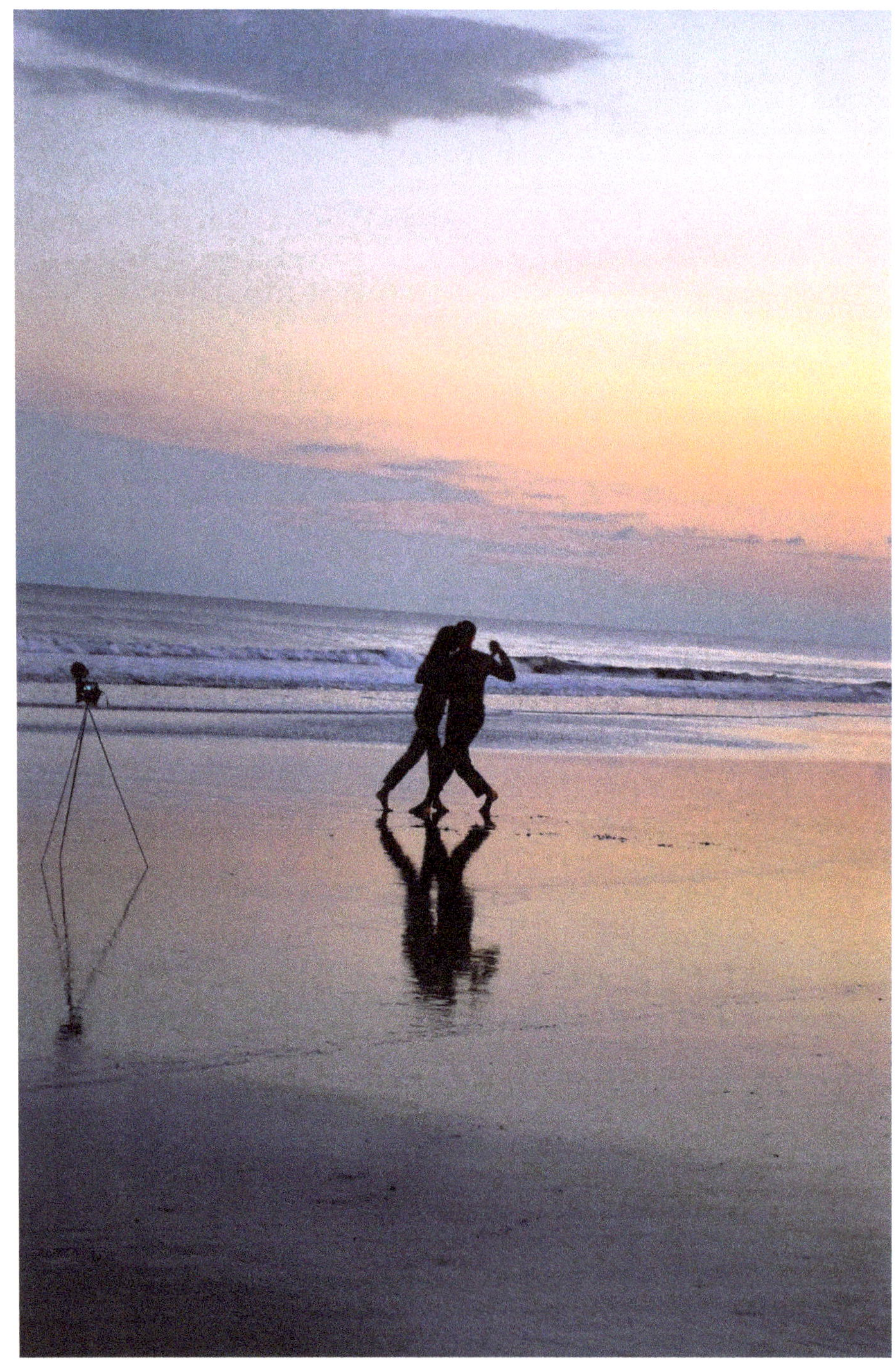

Rhythms

In a close embrace,
they dance the tango
gliding across
heliotrope
and pumpkin-hued
shores.

Swaying
counterclockwise.
Sashaying
figure eights.
Twisting,
courting,
as legs pass
each other.

Her feet keep measure
with his.
Slim bodies
form
fluid rhythms
enraptured
by the sea's harmony.

The separation
of space between
thighs and calves
form diamond shapes
in moist
reflections,
and smoldering
architecture
encouraged by grace.

Toes point.
Ankles arch.
Forelimbs lift,
kick . . .
flirt
like flamingos.
Leaning
Into her heart.

A close embrace –
they dance
the Argentine Tango.

The View from #20 Bella Vista

Dawn gilds
the horizon
as the ferry boat sleeps,
eager to embrace
wide-eyed voyagers
embarking
on a day of discovery.

Loons sail
aloft
alerting,
"All awake!
All awake!"
while a ship's bell
resonates
within call.

Waves
ripple and lap
the tired bones
of a winding
boardwalk.

Estivant pines
hug
the somber inlet,
creating safe
passage
for anglers returning
from a sailor's delight
sky,
spinning
tales of hope,
of the "one that got away."

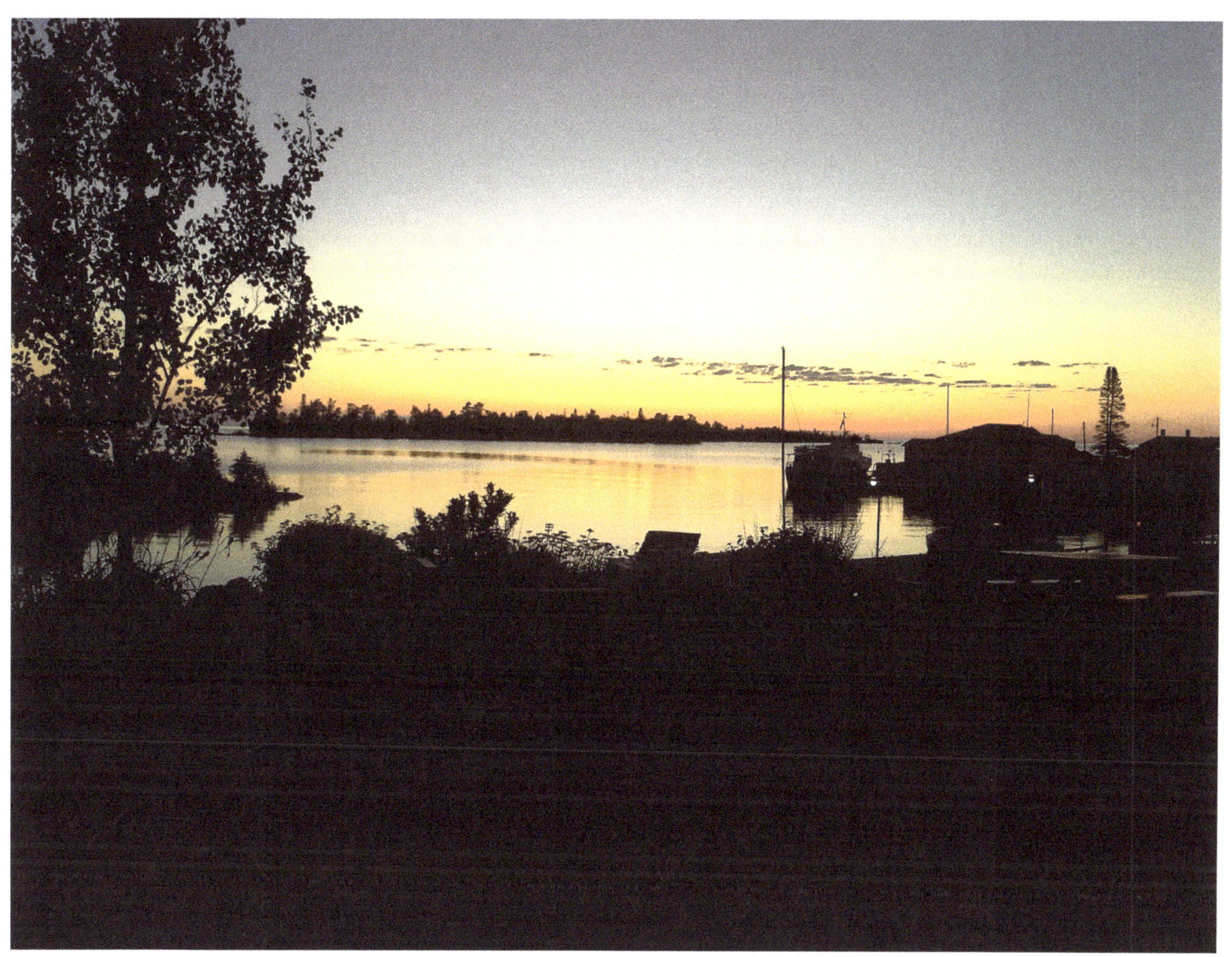

To the Seashore

Barefoot,
we amble the long,
narrow path
through
scratchy vegetation
and rye dune grass,
sometimes cutting
precious paws
and tender heels.

I follow,
camera in tow,
as my Lover,
Red Dog,
and Pretty Dog
run enthusiastically
to reach the final hill
to the beach.

Selecting a spot
for sitting,
I brush sand
from driftwood
bleached by the sun
and worn by the tides.
My toes
dig deep in
the chilly granules.

Lover searches
the seashore
for crystalline agates,
inspecting,
bending,
asking,
"Is this one?"
Casting back
imperfections . . .

Red Dog watches,
pensive,
eyeing his best friend.

Shore birds
glide overhead
riding a gust
of wind.

Red Dog –
always
on guard
for me
and Pretty Dog.

Pretty Dog
shows off
ice blue eyes
and freckled snout.

Paws crossed,
she rests quietly
near my feet.

Cool,
gusty,
breezes
lift her coal black
and ivory fur
upward.

I huddle my chin
beneath the grey cotton
warm-up jacket
as the lake takes on characteristics
of a wild, untamed
ocean.
Waves crashing.
A fog horn sounds
in the distance . . .

Sun sets a golden cornucopia
of caramels and beiges
on the horizon
as silhouettes
of Lover
and Red Dog
appear in my
picture frame.

Quickly,
the sphere
dips low.
A circle of blood orange
blaze
and midnight blue
fill my vision.

The four of us
move swiftly
to an observation spot
atop the summit.
White Adirondack chairs
nestle in sleepy dunes.

We garner one last look
of the time
Between day and night.

And breathe
crisp,
clean,
unfettered
air.

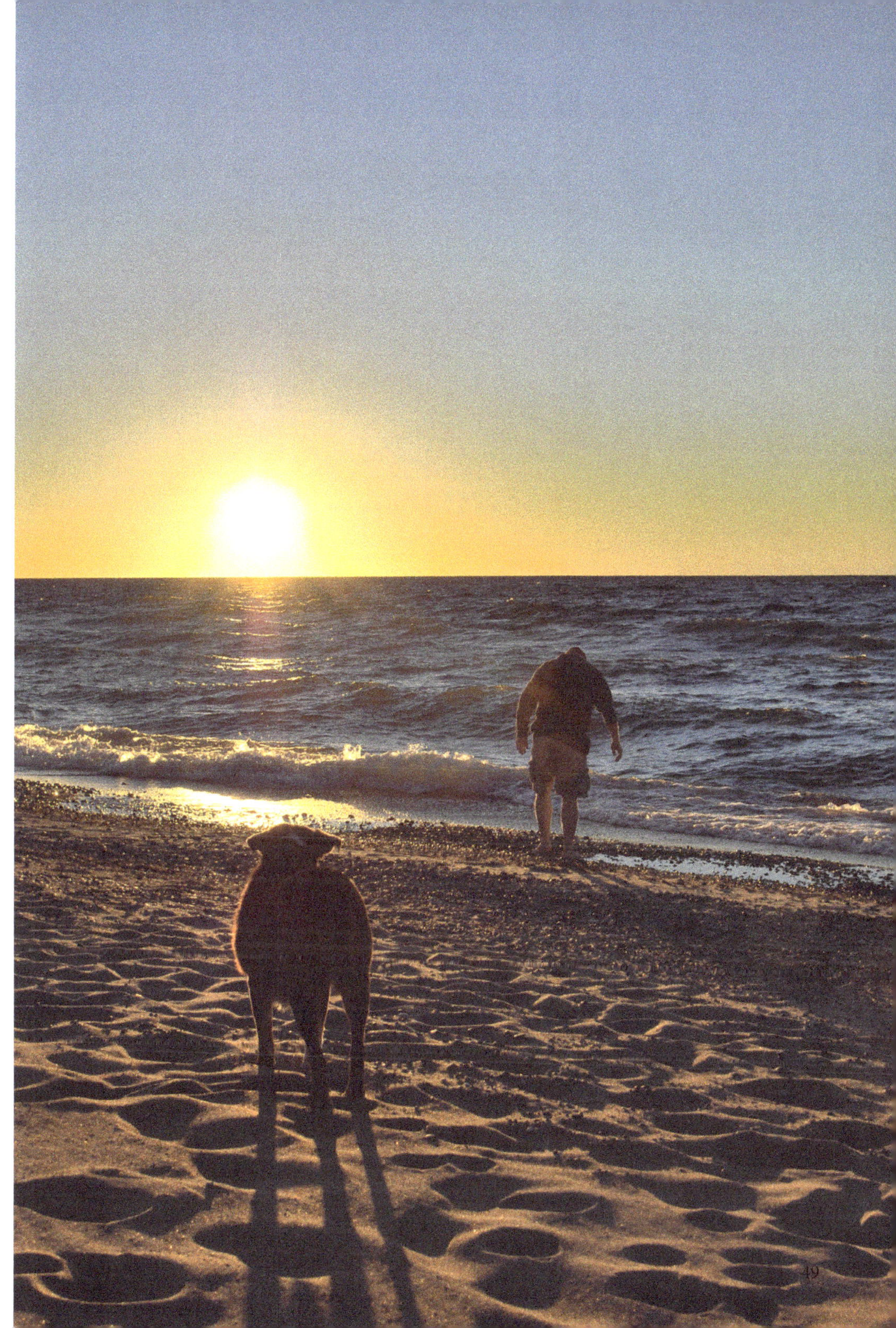

Carolina Delight

Waves crashing,
Children splashing,
That's Folly at night.

Distant lights glimmer.
Shifting sands shimmer.
That's Folly at night.

Neon signs illuminate.
The weekend can't wait!
That's Folly at night.

A stroll down the Pier . . .
Bring your fishing gear.
That's Folly at night.

Snuggling on the beach,
Stars are within reach.
That's Folly at night.

Whatever the weather
Carolina forever!
My Folly by night.

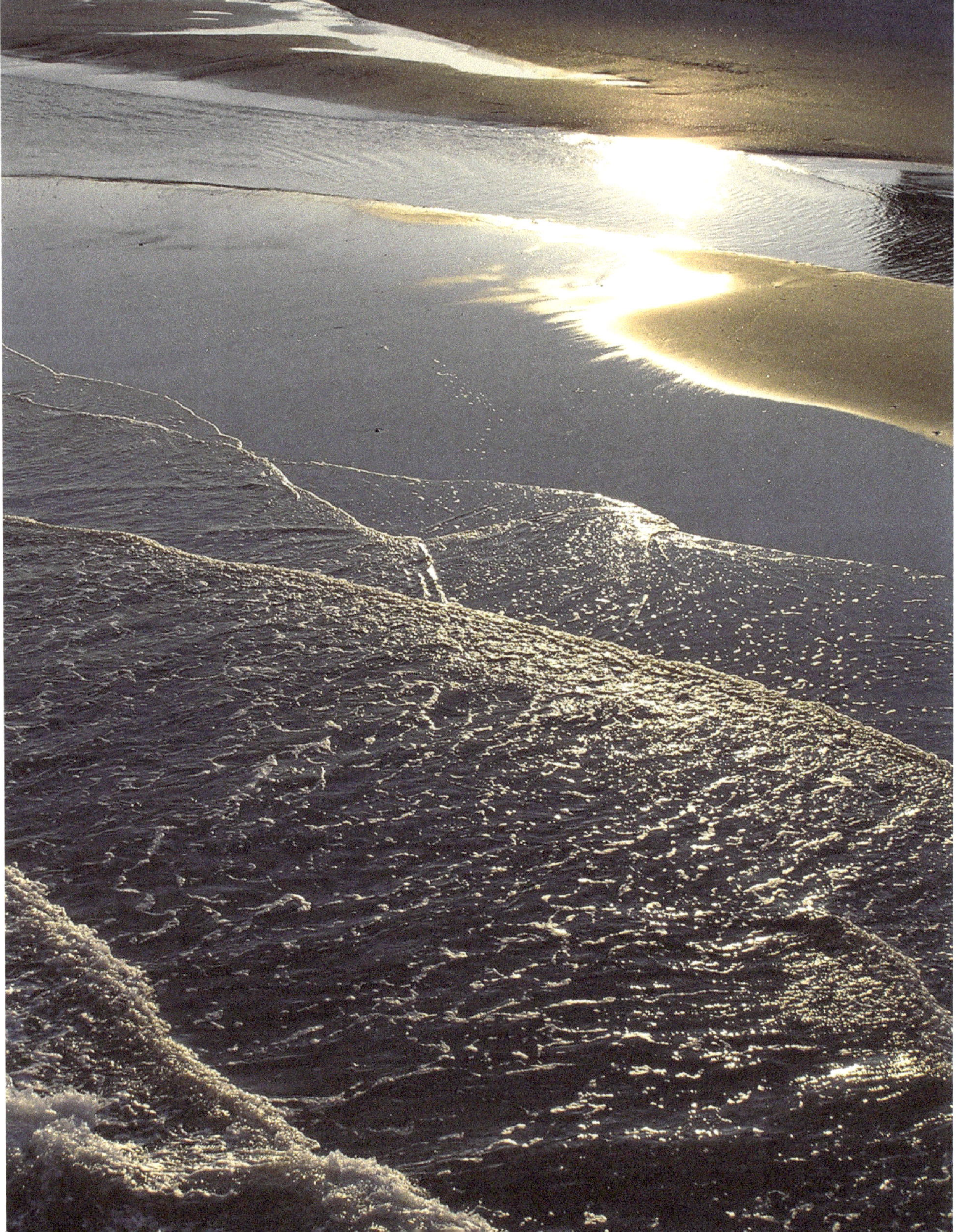

Liquid Dancing

The glistening water
Reflects from the sun
Hints of golden maize and beige gray
In this late morning swelter,
With ripples
That form parallel
To the sand
Similar to
An Escher drawing.

Section Three

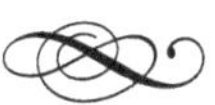

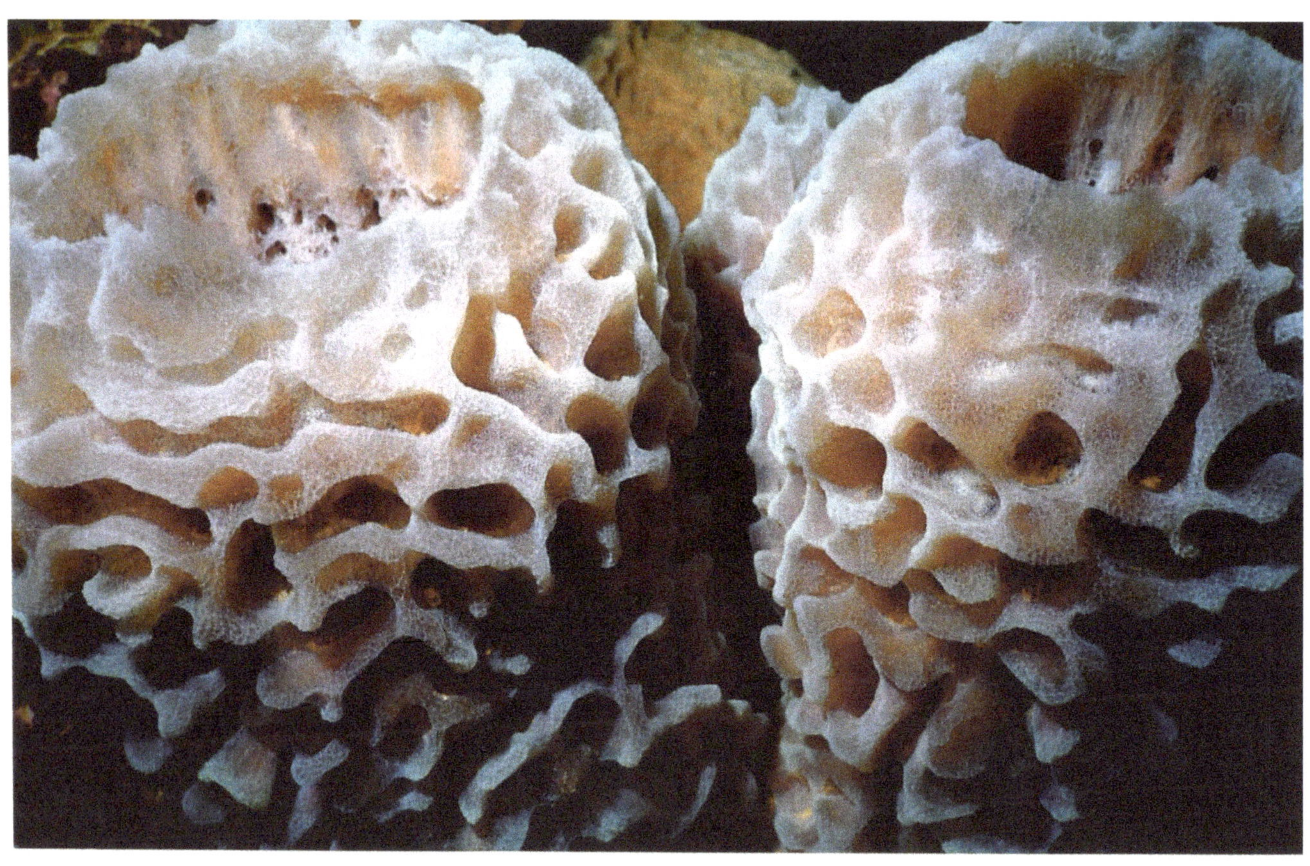

The Wall

I dive down
deep,
compressed,
enveloped
by the ocean's palette –
cerulean,
delphinium
and indigo blues.

In a ballet with the sea,
I float effortlessly
hovering
over
gargantuan
bubble gum pink
barrel sponges,
lavender sea fans,
and aubergine
rope corals,
while breathing
from an apparatus
that somehow seems
foreign
to me.

Never ending
is the ocean's
sensational
breadth,
and unimaginable
depth.

Mere feet
from my buoyant
exoskeleton
two hammerheads
navigate stealthily
riding the crest
of the Wall.

In the chasm,
fluidity of thoughts
rush
my cerebral cortex
in a moment
of clarity.

Suddenly,
I feel freer
than I've
ever
felt
in my life.

The Time Before Night

A single seagull
bobs
delicately,
upon cool,
glassy
apricot waters,
and kisses
smudged
pewter greys,
streaks of plum,
then apricot,
then plum
again . . .

Silhouettes
of the island
smile like a panda's eyes –
ever so slightly
squinted,
as day
slips into
the time before
night,
and reality
becomes
a Utopian
dream.

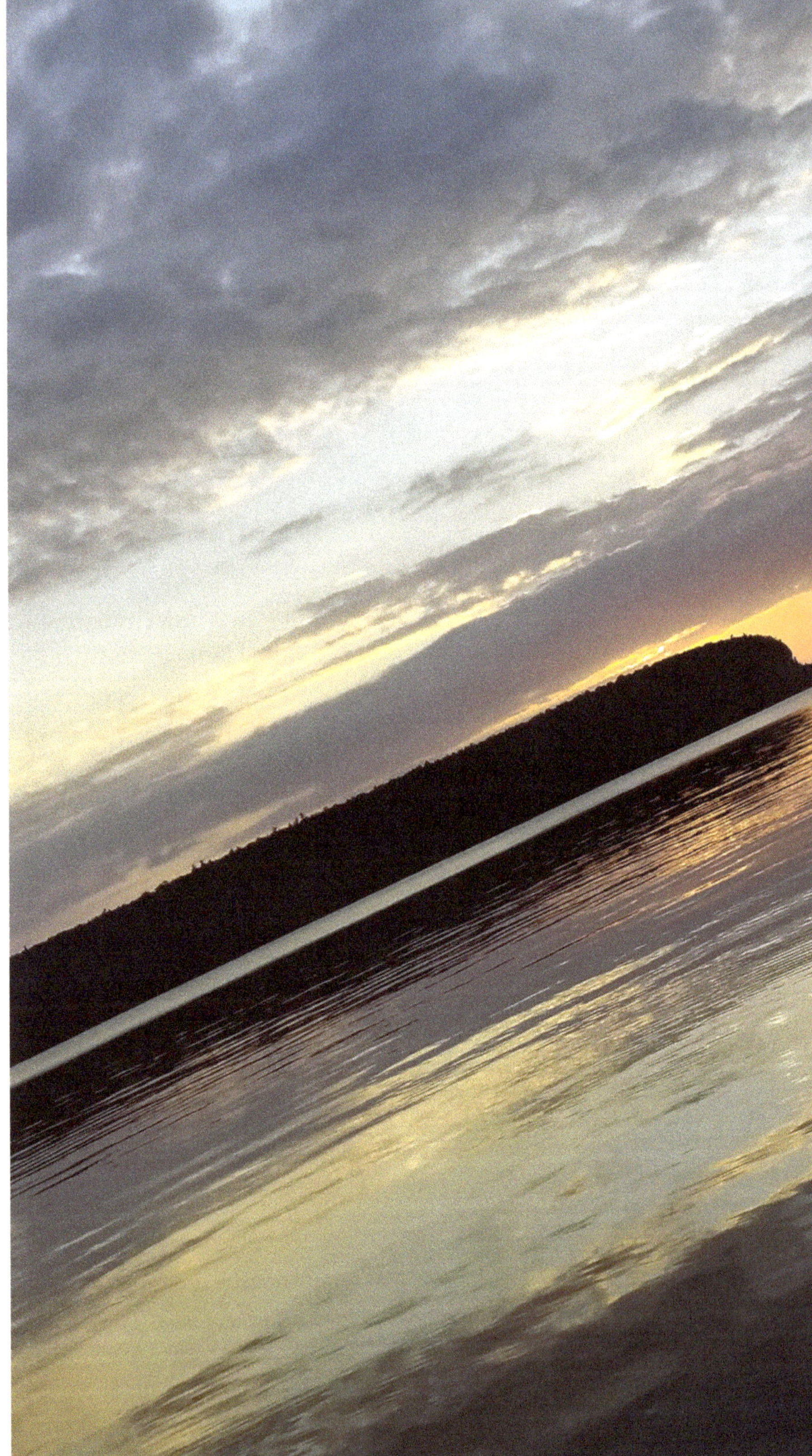

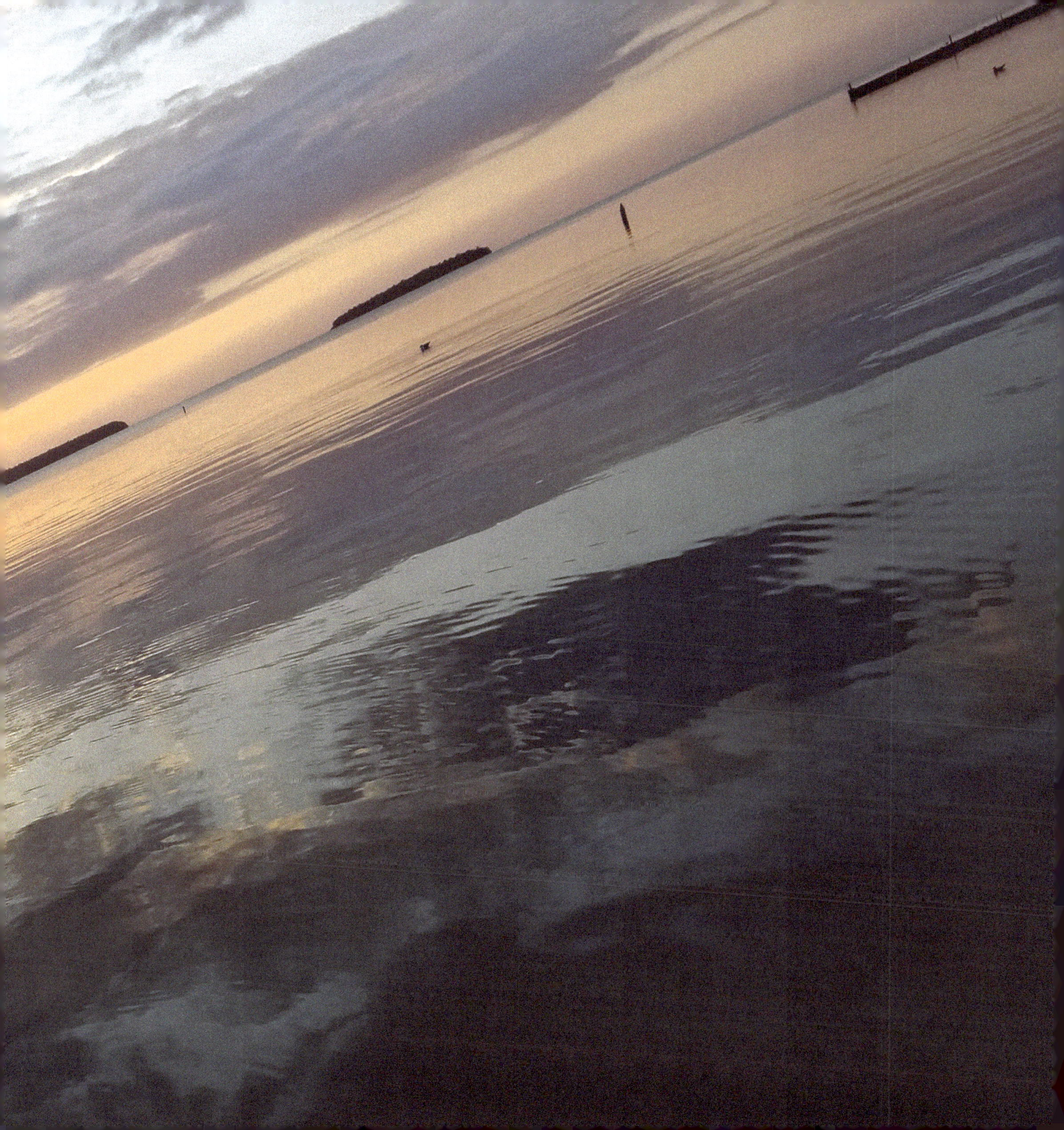

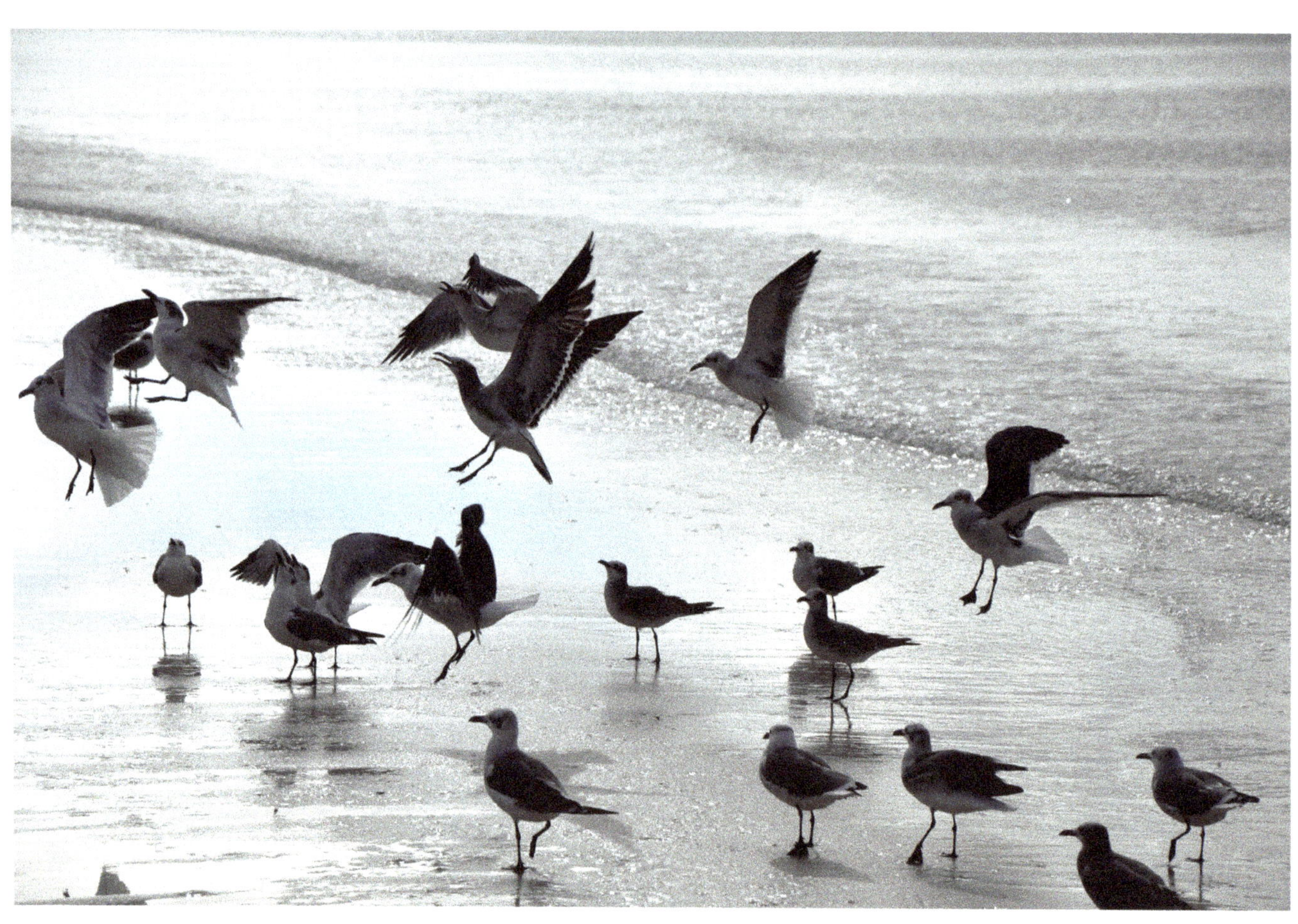

Intangible Vacation

Faded –
the coal black line
on the horizon.

Subsided –
remnants
of a tempestuous storm.

Eyes closed,
the pounding sea
delivers
synchronized waves
pushing boldly
towards me.

Eyes open,
a harvest of green and yellow
sea grasses . . .

The dunes roll gently
to the sand.

A runner jogs in time
as twenty or more
seagulls rest,
basking in the golden sunrise,
reflecting from the wet, yet powdery,
shoreline.

The sky offers
crème fraiche arms
gracefully outstretched
to envelope the atmosphere.

An Egyptian sphinx
appears in the cornflower blue space
between the clouds.

Wait.

Now it's gone.

White birds soar,
littering the sky
and float
like paper airplanes
above the teal-grey ocean.

I sit quietly,
relieved,
that my body
and not my mind
took a necessary
vacation . . .

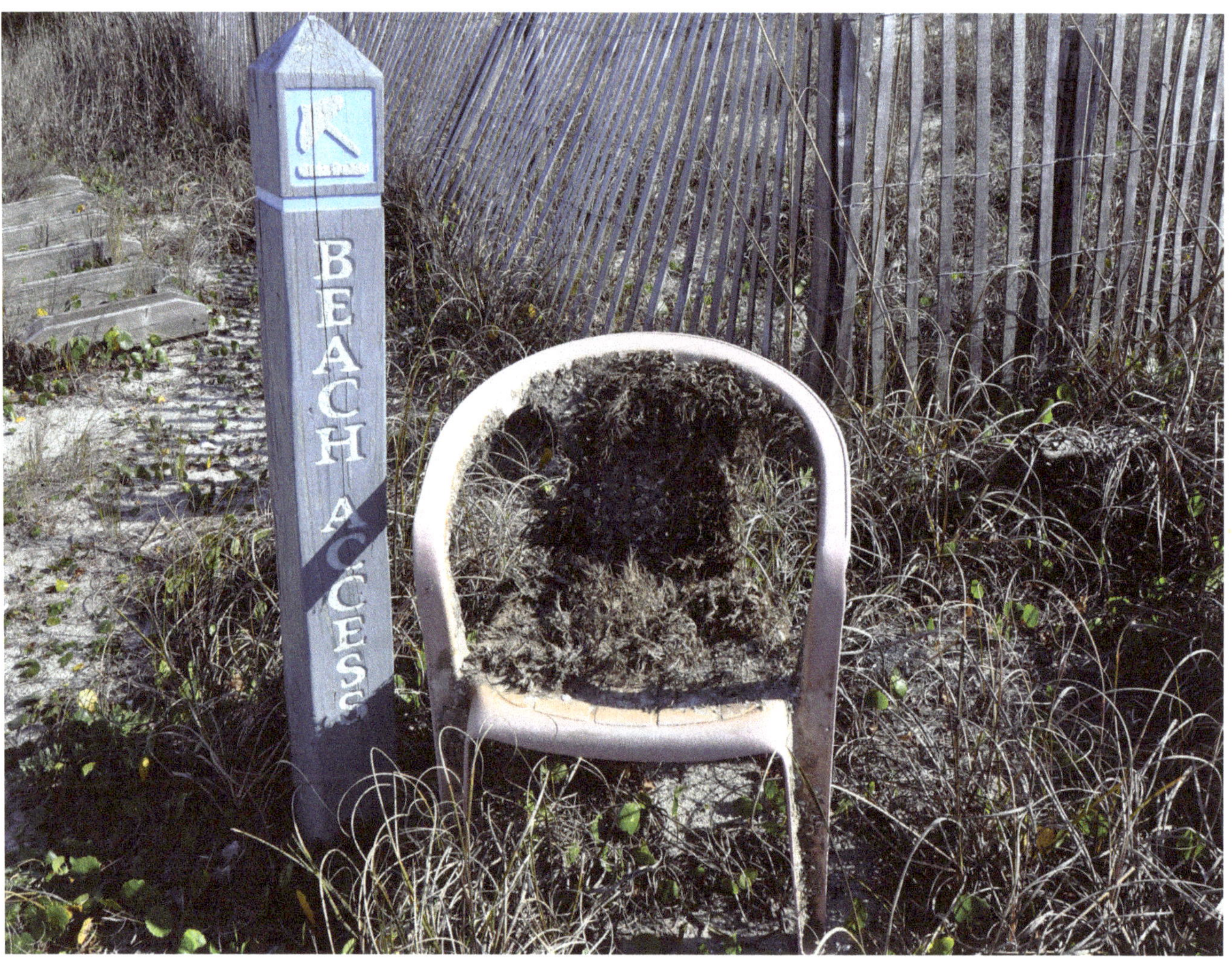
BEACH ACCESS

Ode to Sponge Chair

The sea claimed her.

She settled softly,
in the ocean depths.
Interwoven with the underwater world,
her plant growth sustained
vibrant marine life.

Fish found refuge
in her embrace.

The deep blue
regurgitated her.

A passerby
rescued her.

Curious,
my husband photographed her.

A gentleman
reclaimed her.

And within a few minutes,
a simple
plastic
chair touched four lives,
made us smile,
and no doubt
gave us something to talk about
at least
for awhile . . .

Soul Sister Journey

The leather covered wheel
of the freshly-waxed
licorice red
Mercedes
feels warm to the touch
as the sole of my Raffini sandals
push pedal
to the floor.

Speeding down Cabrillo Highway,
the aroma
of fresh spring air,
surf, grass,
and perspiration
penetrate
our senses.

Wind billows
through
loosely-knotted
scarves – silk flowered
magenta, canary,
securing neatly-tucked
tangled
locks.

Vintage,
leather seats
soften,
baked by
California
rays.

I steer the convertible
to an overlook –
windsurfers
clad in slick,
black neoprene
navigate the area
where the waves break.

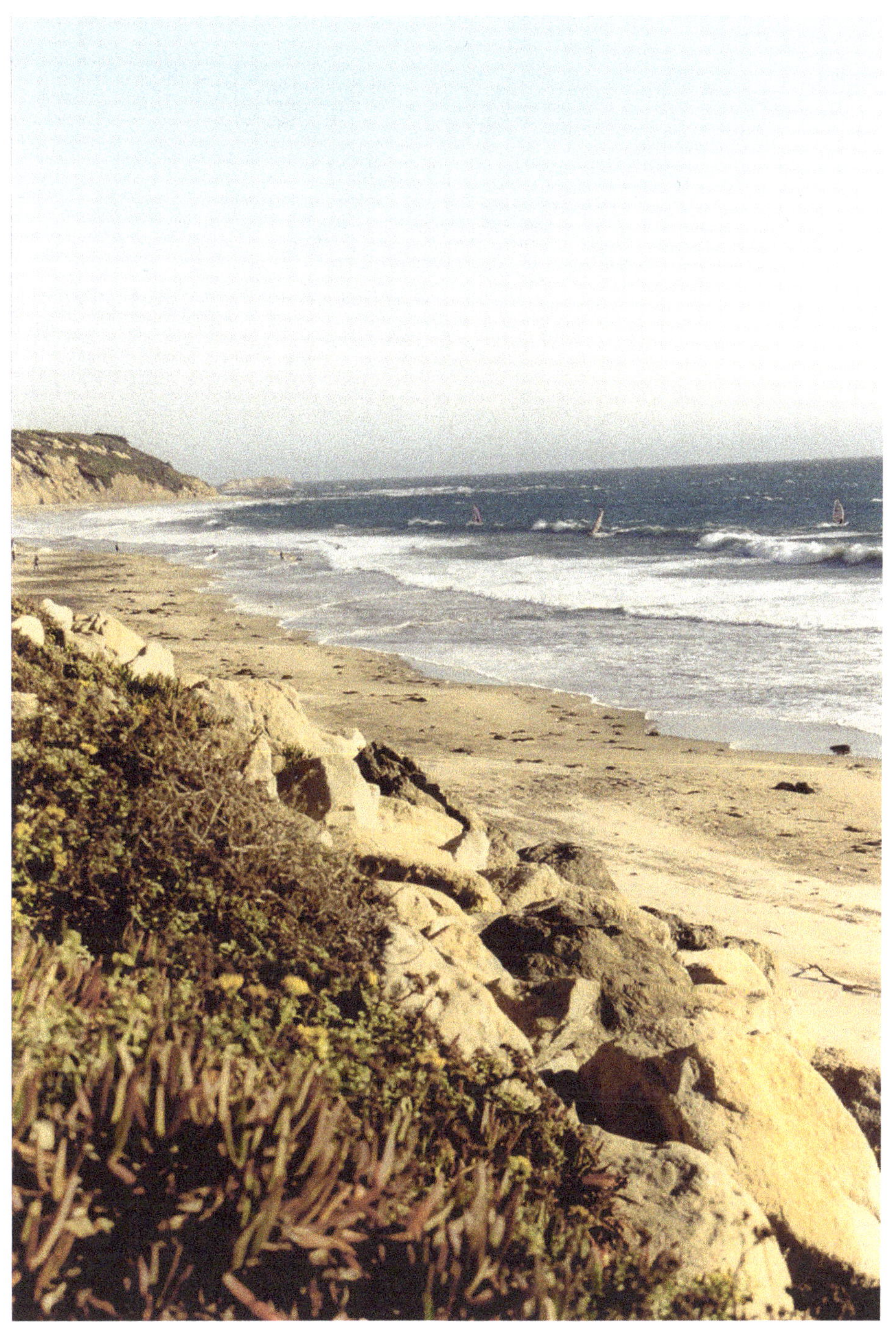

Island Girl

Creamy
biscotti-hued
tresses
hug
a sleek,
wet,
athletic
frame.

Sand sprinkled
round
soulful
doe-like eyes
compliment
her cinnamon
complexion.

A blemish,
pale pink in color,
dime-sized,
lay
just above
her snout.

She is
one hundred percent
dog.

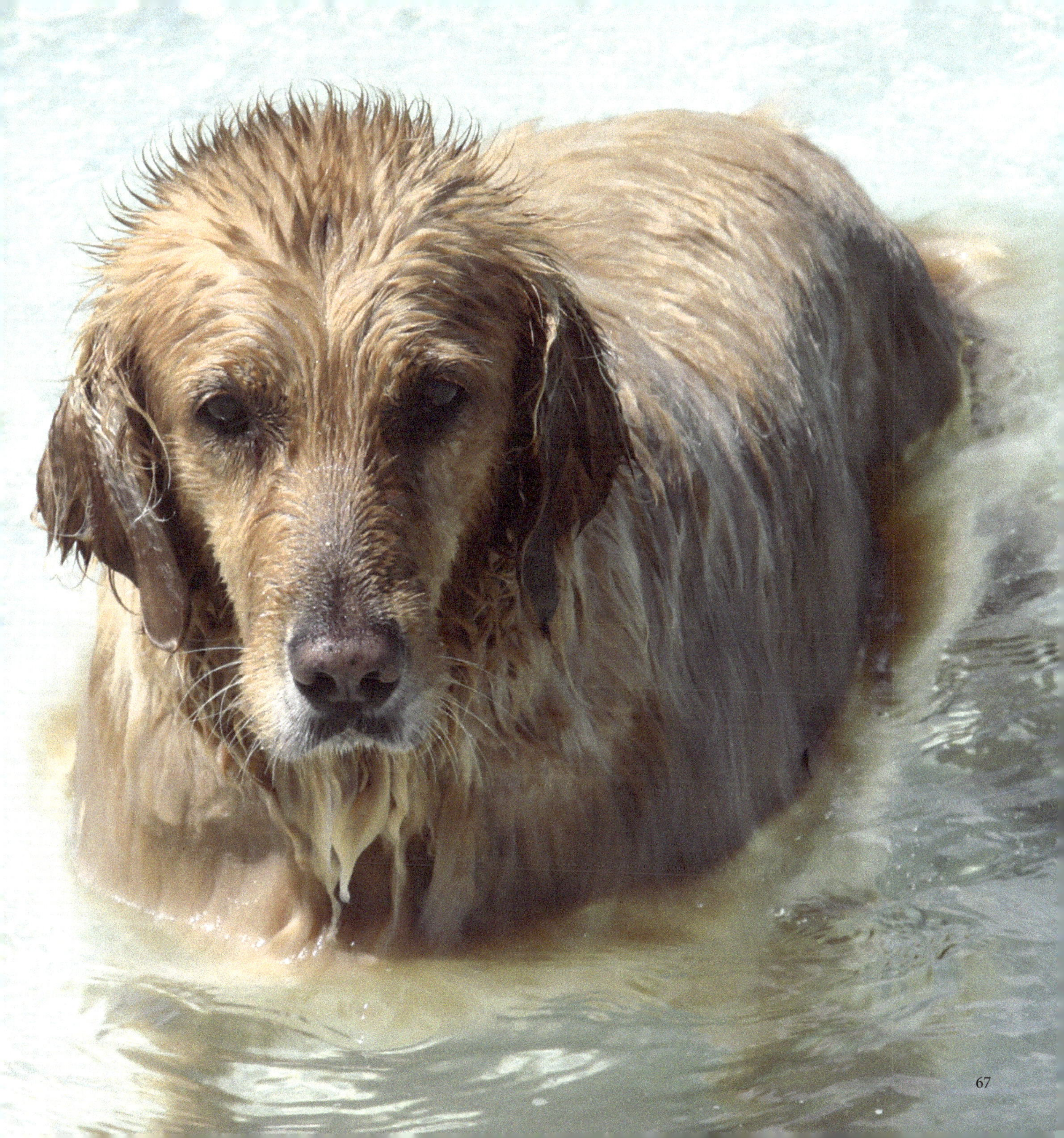

Red Dog's Observations

Red Dog
intently studies
the harvest landscape,
listening
to the cardinal's felicity,
and echoes
of coyote's waling,
murmuring
across
the bucolic meadow.

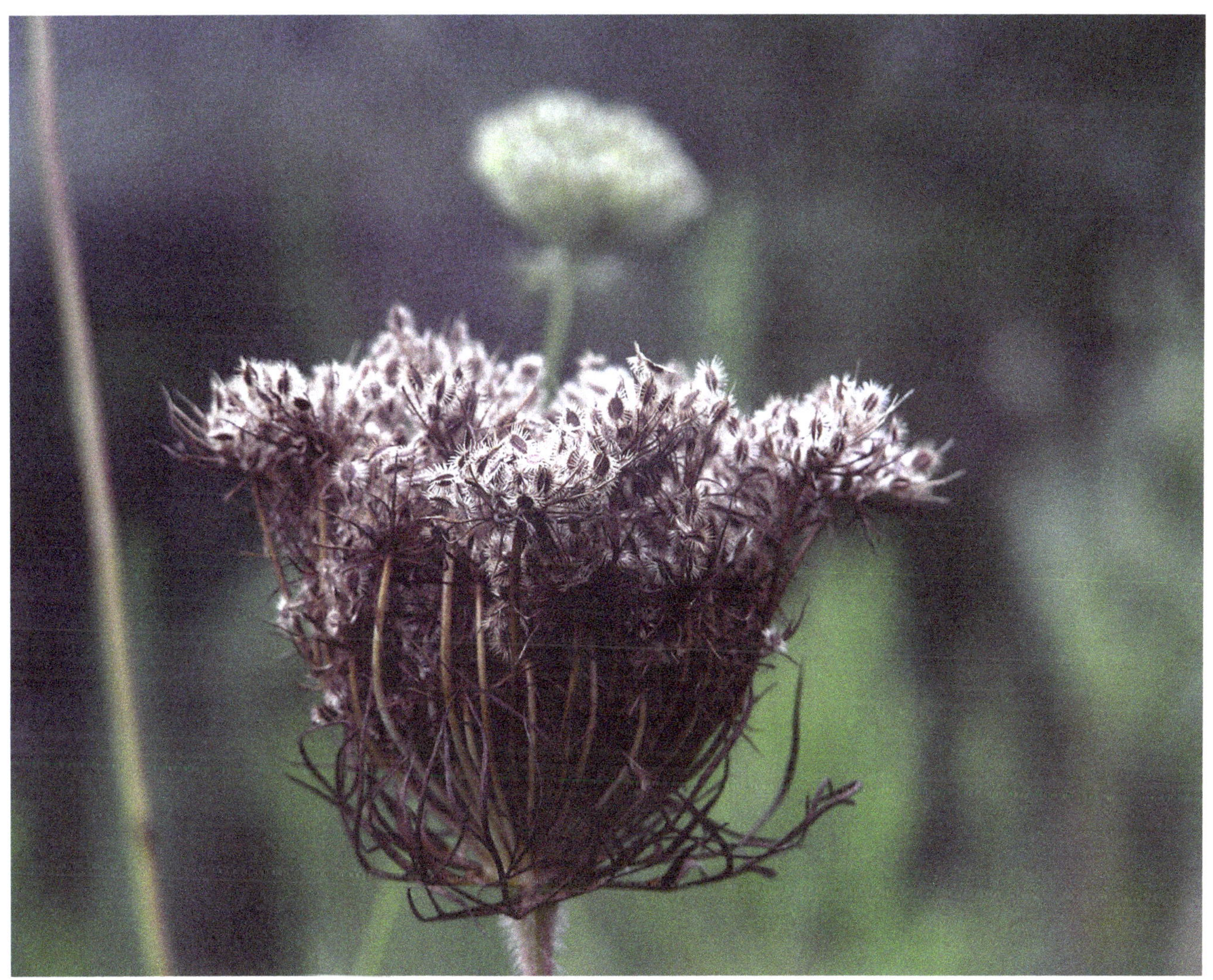

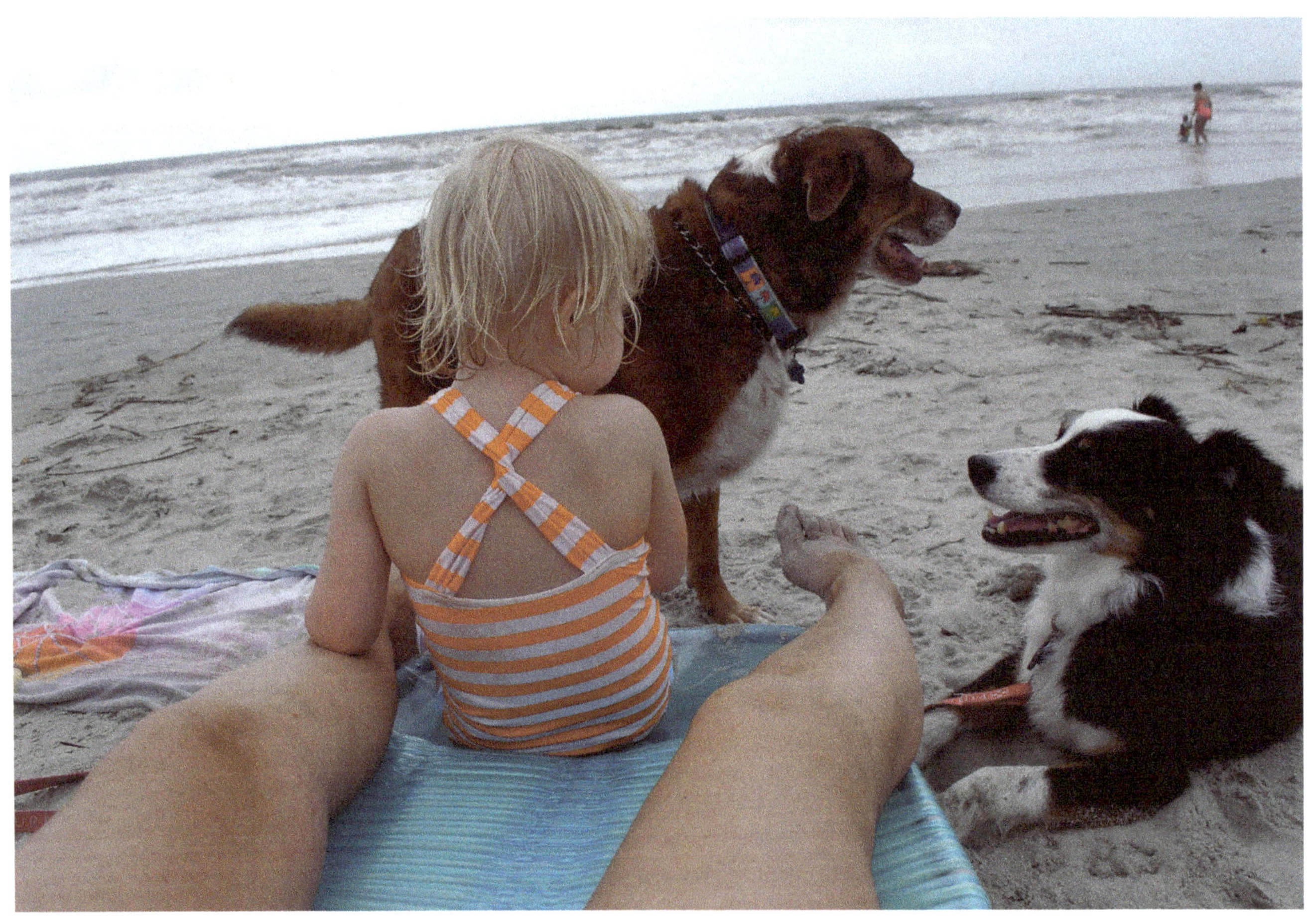

Mondays in October

Worried minds
and tense bodies
melt away
with the simple brush
of an ocean breeze
across eburnean cheeks.

Little girls named Remy
donning jacinthe and white-striped
bathing suits
with messy blonde hair,
sandy toes,
and sticky fingers
sipping strawberry-kiwi
pouch drinks
plop down
on opaque aqua
spaghetti-webbed
chaise lounges
become your best friend
at the beach,
on Mondays
in October.

Encounter in the Abyss 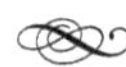

What a pretty girl
long and lean,
as she slips
through the water
in the company of
two bar jacks.

Four gill slits
above her pectoral fin
sit in
perfect
alignment
with her eye.

Several scars
adjacent to her
lower
furrows,
and a small
gash
above her fins
reveal her past.

She′s as gracious
as she is
graceful.

Hues of gray-violet,
silver
blend with
delicate tones
of pale 'bruised' yellow
on her sleek
slick
skin.

Beautiful
as a dusky
ocean sunset,
she hovers
in the abyss
watching us,
ever cautiously . . .

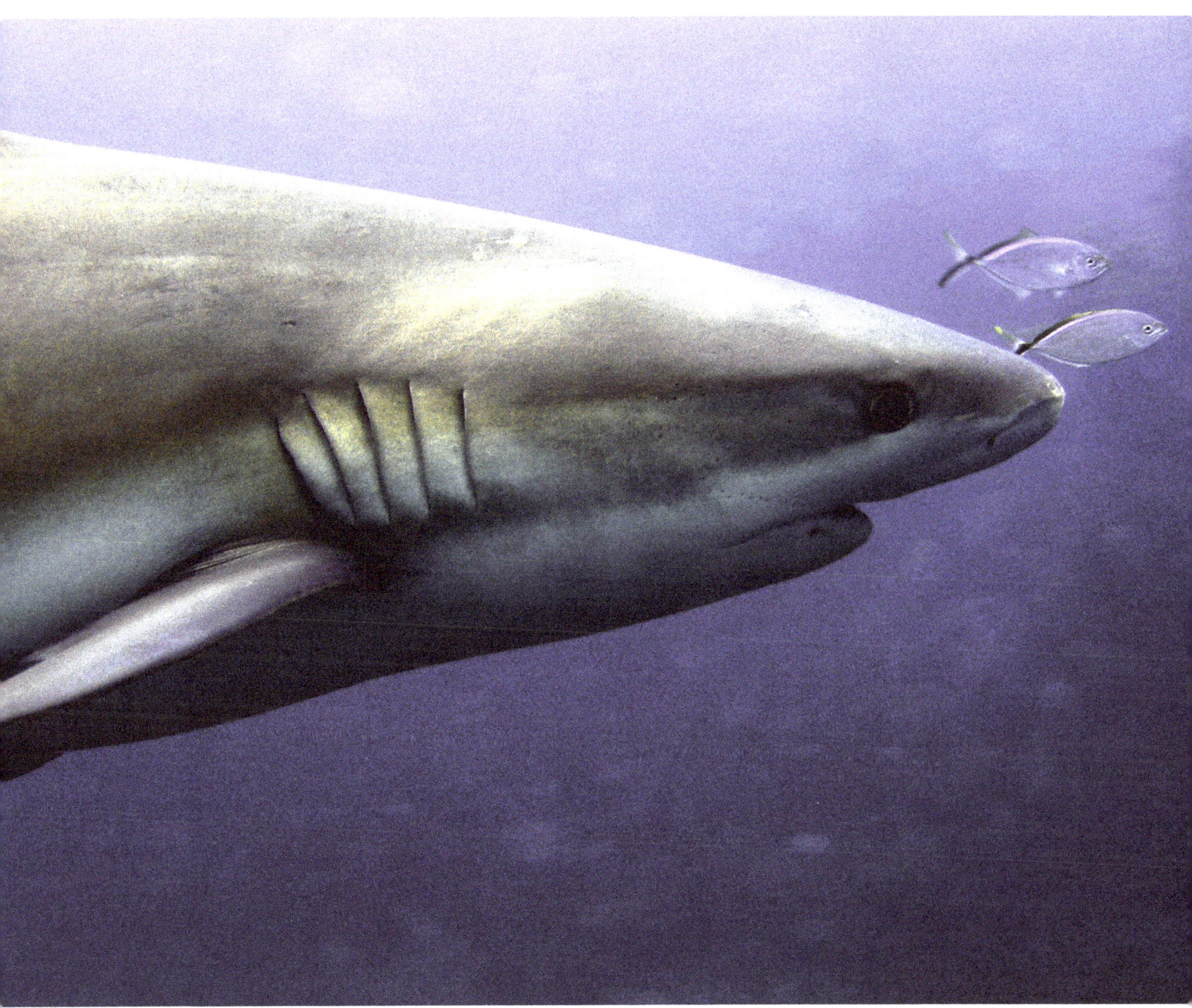

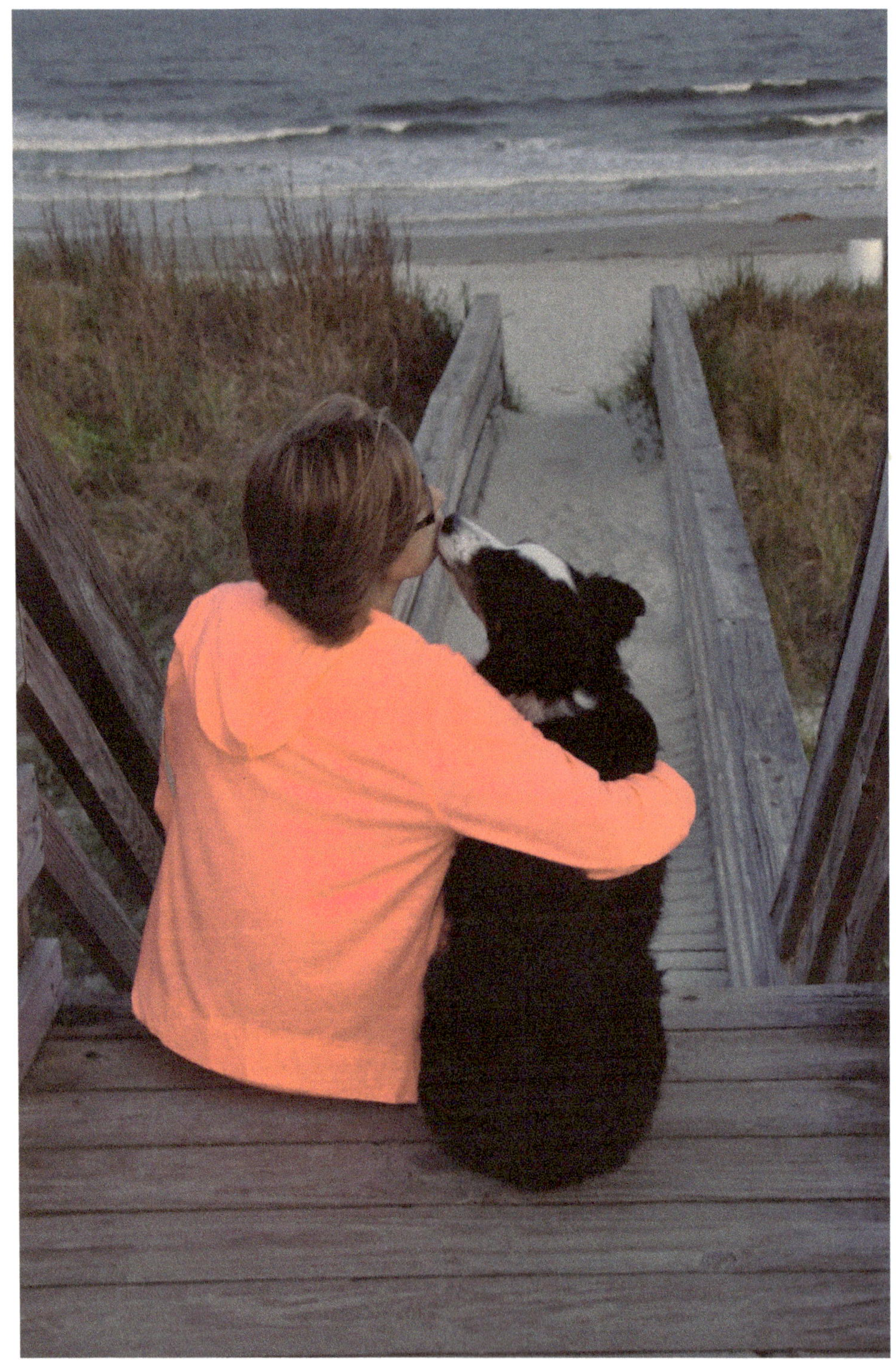

Sabrina

She smiles at me
with undying affection.

Those glacier-blue eyes
entangle my heart
and steal
my
life . . .

Westerly
breezes
lift a tuft
of lustrous
sable fur upward,
lightly touching
my tawny cheek.

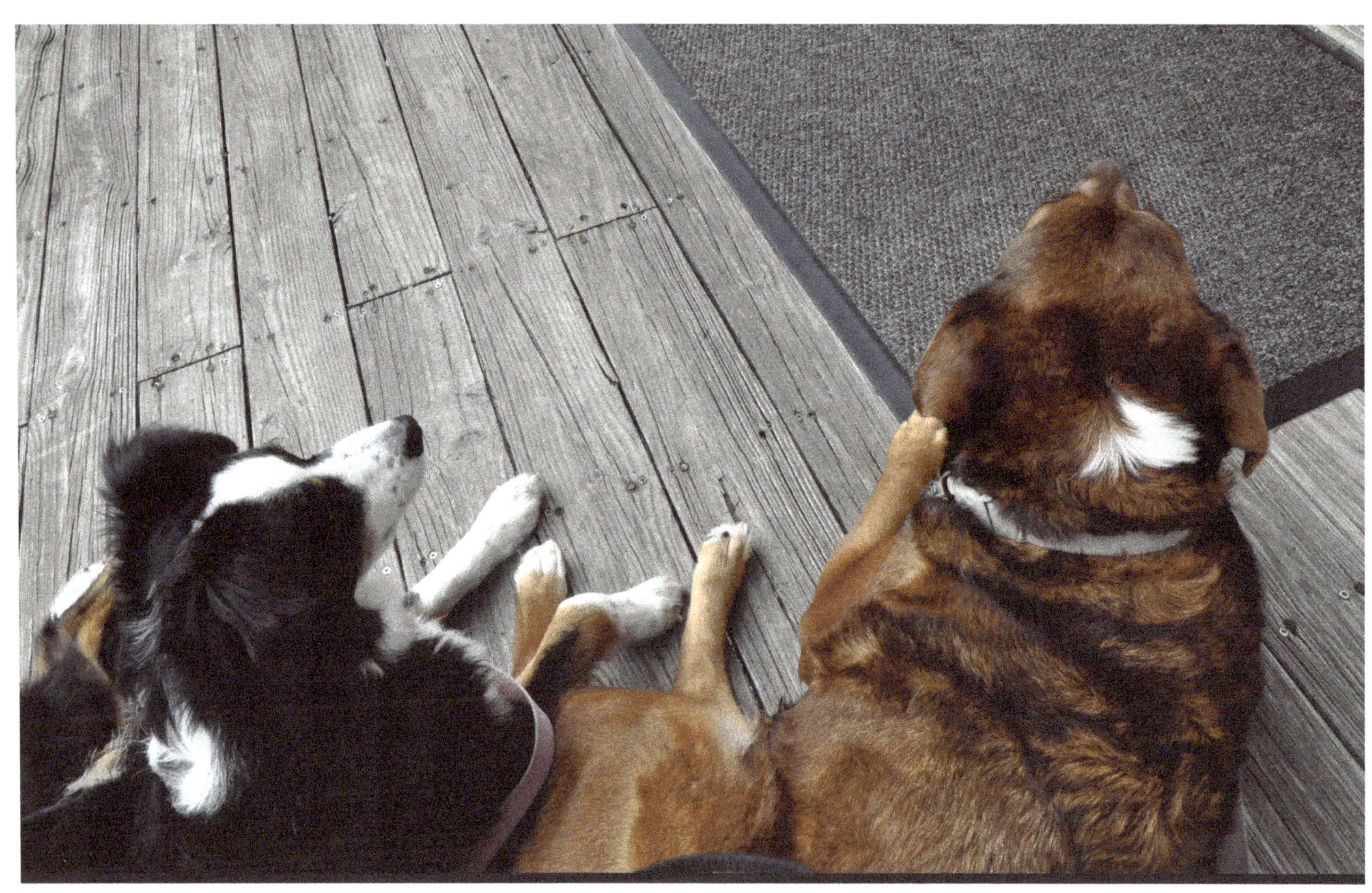

Salty Dogs Morning

The ring-clink of bicycle bells
chime
on charming
Main Street,
blending
with giggling chatter
of rosy-bronzed
cheeked
children
whizzing past
the beach
bungalow.

High atop
a stilted foundation,
Red Dog
and Pretty Dog
repose
astride
knobby knotted rugs,
paws crossed,
intuitively
observing
passersby
and the offing.

Nature's bounty –
sea, sand, sky,
tarries
outside
their door.

The Drifter

Not far in the distance
I notice an old tree, now driftwood,
with branches
reaching out to a cornflower blue sky
and white-streaked cotton clouds.

The image of a beach bungalow
appears in my head,
with sounds of laughter,
lazy days
in the sun,
peaceful ocean breezes,
smoky barbeques at dusk
and a warm
crackling fire
at night.

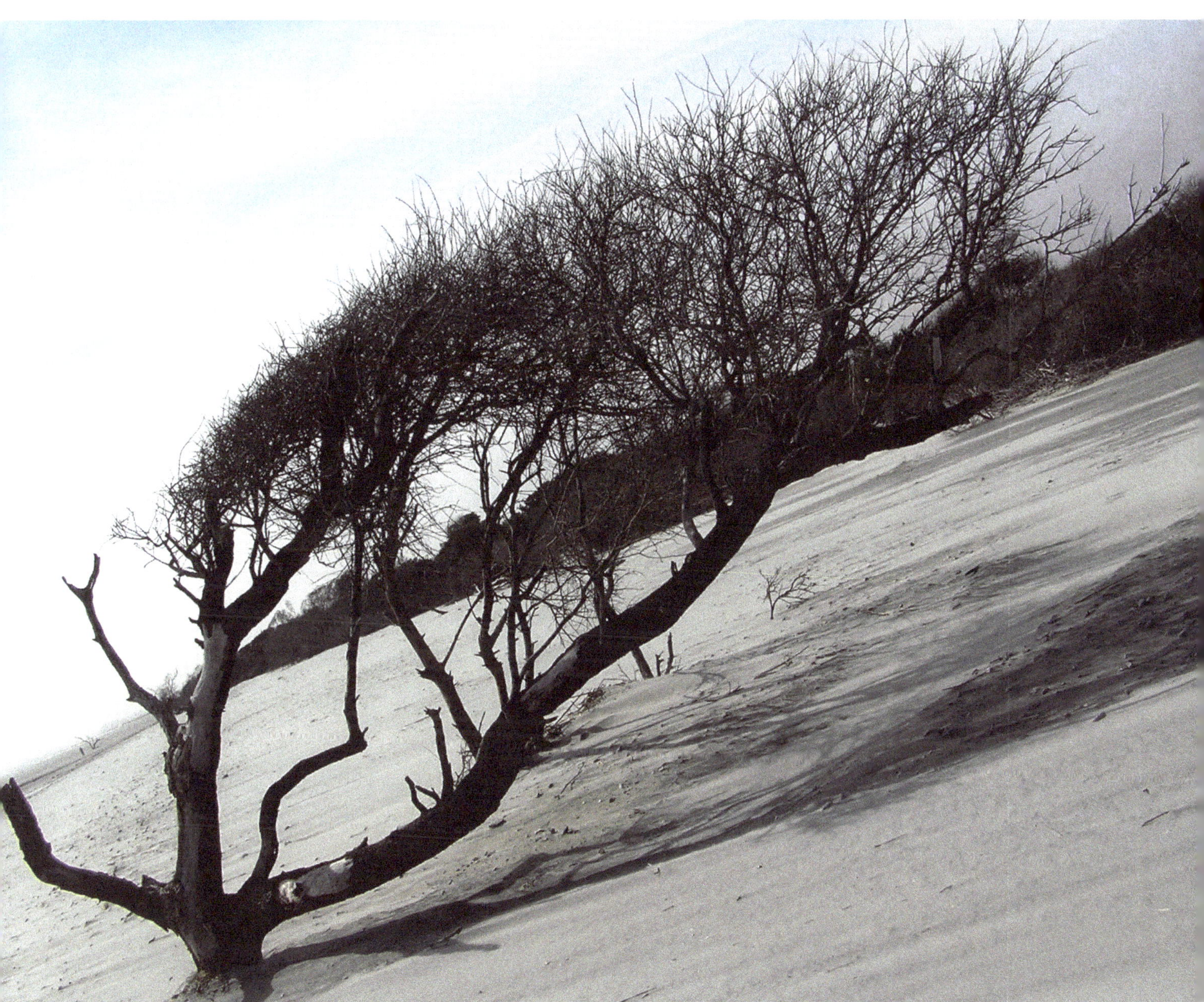

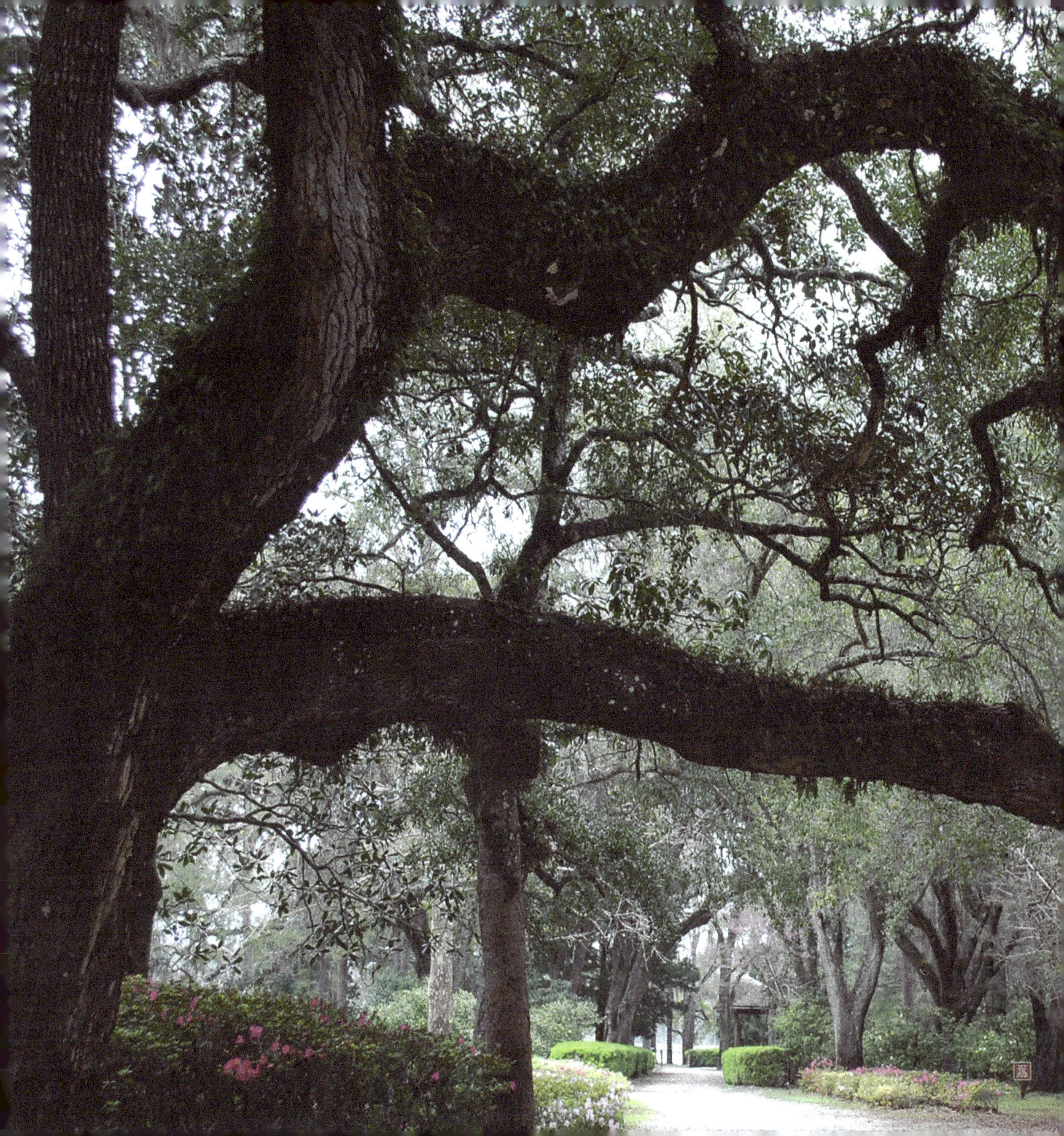

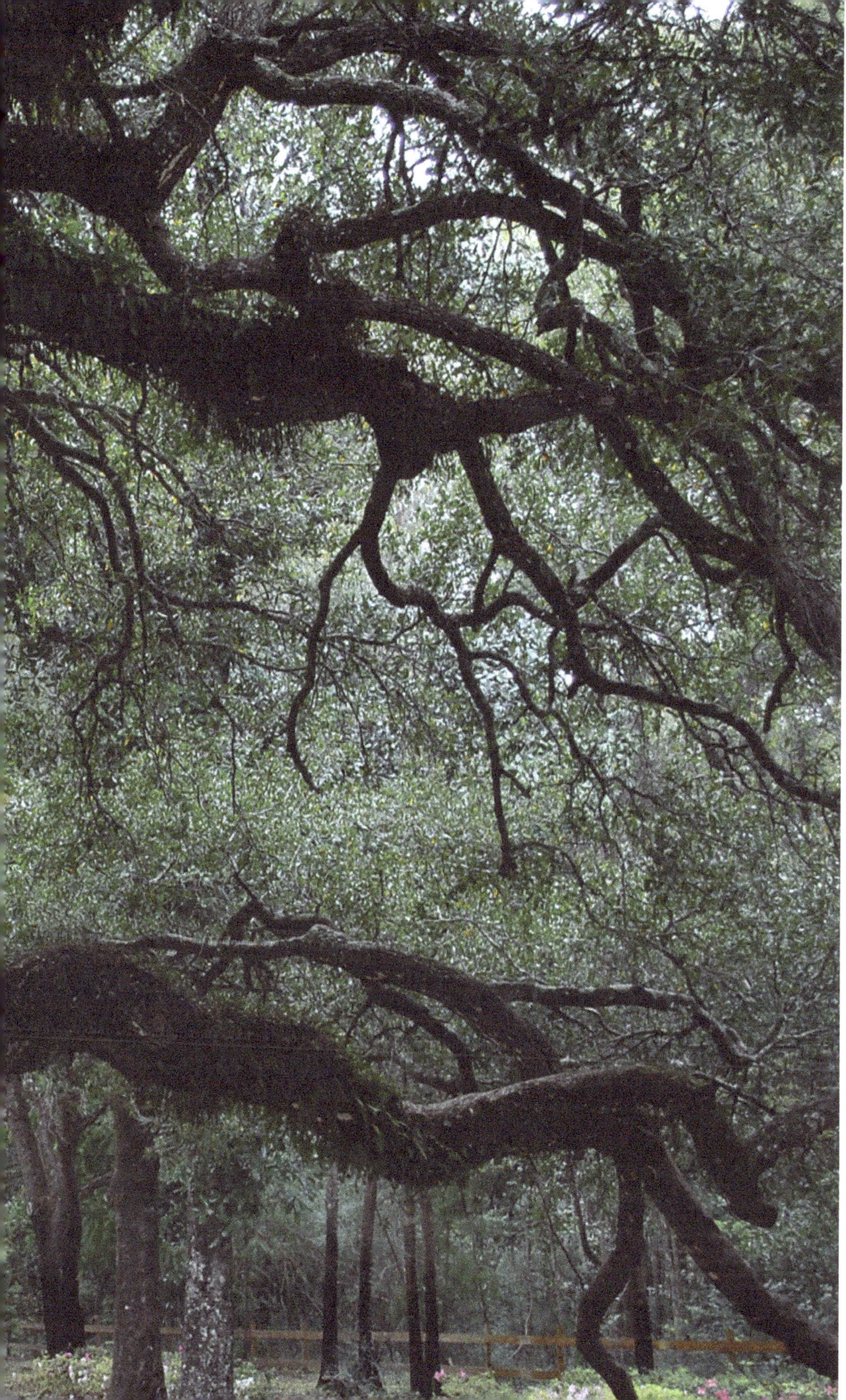

Their Fourth Date

They rendezvous
at the fork in the road
where the tangled oak
casts shadows
upon the weathered
wood bench.

Embracing,
his supple black leathers
press firmly
against her
Hounds tooth skirt
and snug,
ebony tights.

Circadian rhythms
are reset.

The sweltering sun
is pregnant
with heat.

Fully cognizant,
adrenalin rushes through
a crimson river
of veins,
as tides
ebb and flow,
to the ever-changing
sea.

Layers of fabric
walk a thin tightrope
between
protection
and
passion.

Be-ing

Banana-eating
baseball cap wearers,
barefoot bikini clad
buxom brunettes,
buff runners with blistered big toes,
boogie-boarding
bronze-skinned boys,
Bird Island bound bicyclists,
Dasani bottle-carrying
Bernese Mountain Dogs,
Boxers, border collies, and bull terriers,
Blue-eyed blonde-haired bouncing babies
in beach buggies
holding plastic buckets,
box kite fliers,
baby boomers bearing bottles of Bordeaux wine,
belching beer-bellied boasters,
meander the beach,
basking in the sun's brilliance,
with bleeding tooth shells underfoot.

Billowy clouds and shrimp boats
bedizen the seascape.

Blanketing the dunes –
bitter lemon hued
blooming wild roses,
And beguiling
beach plums.

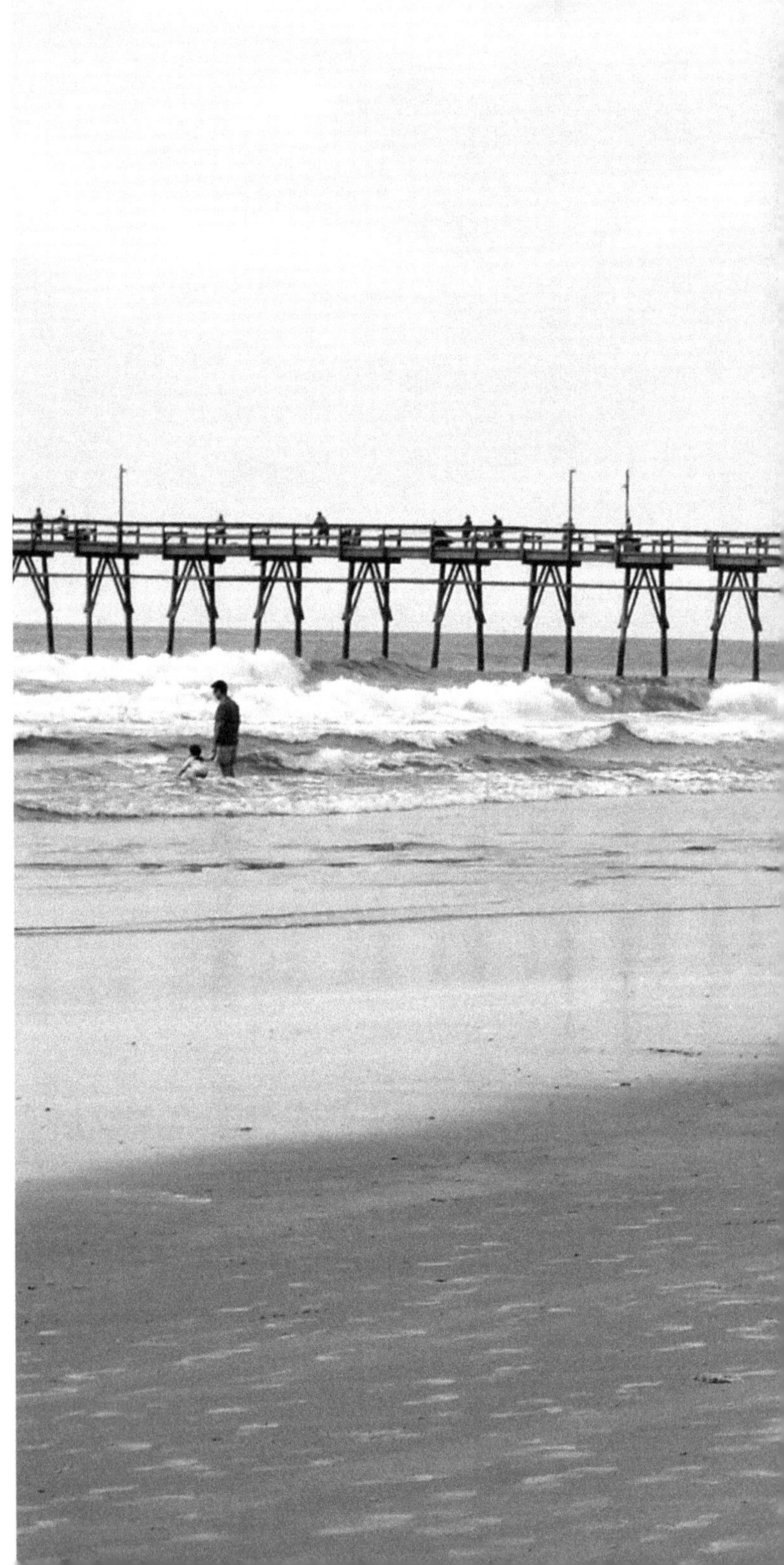

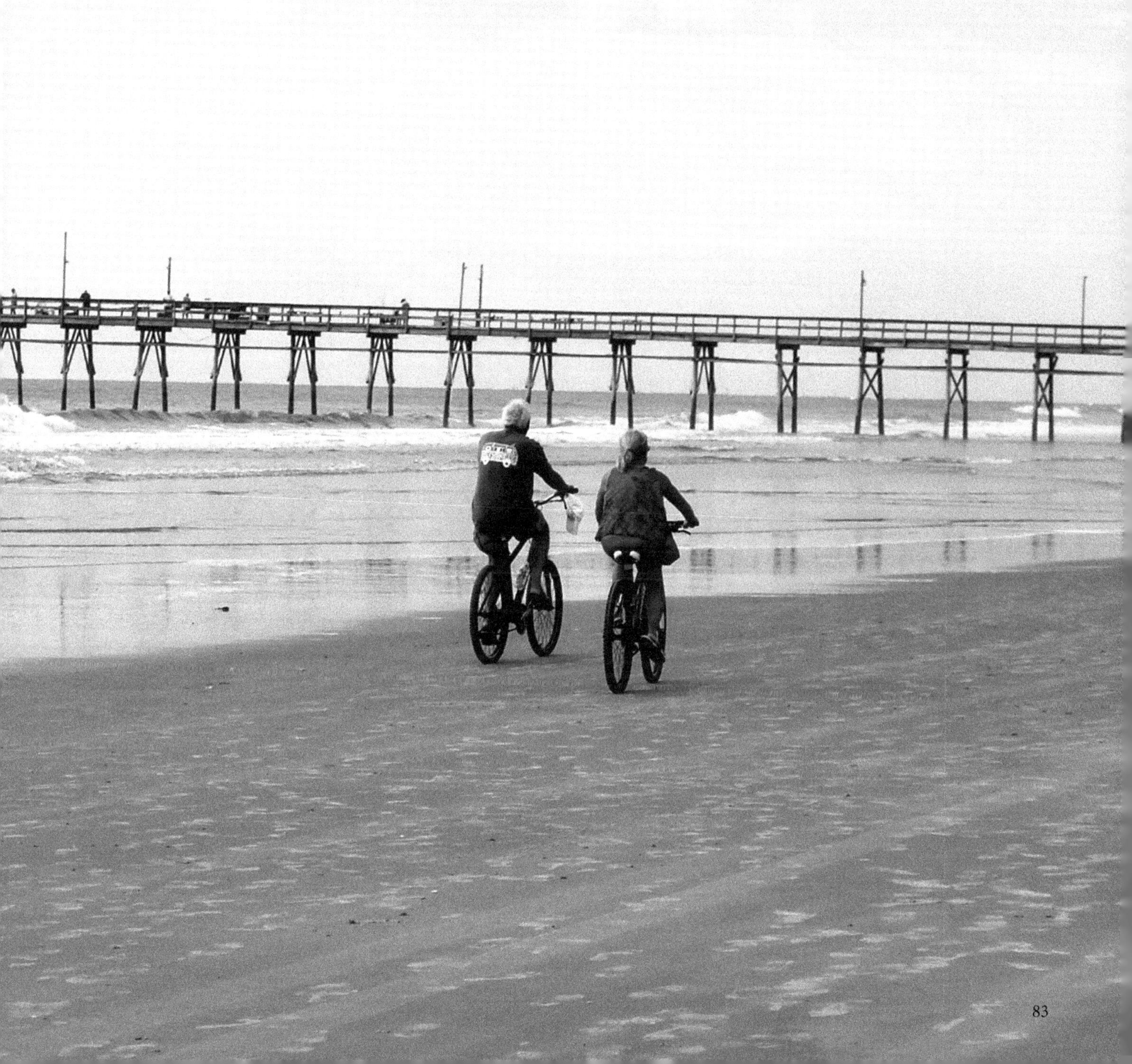

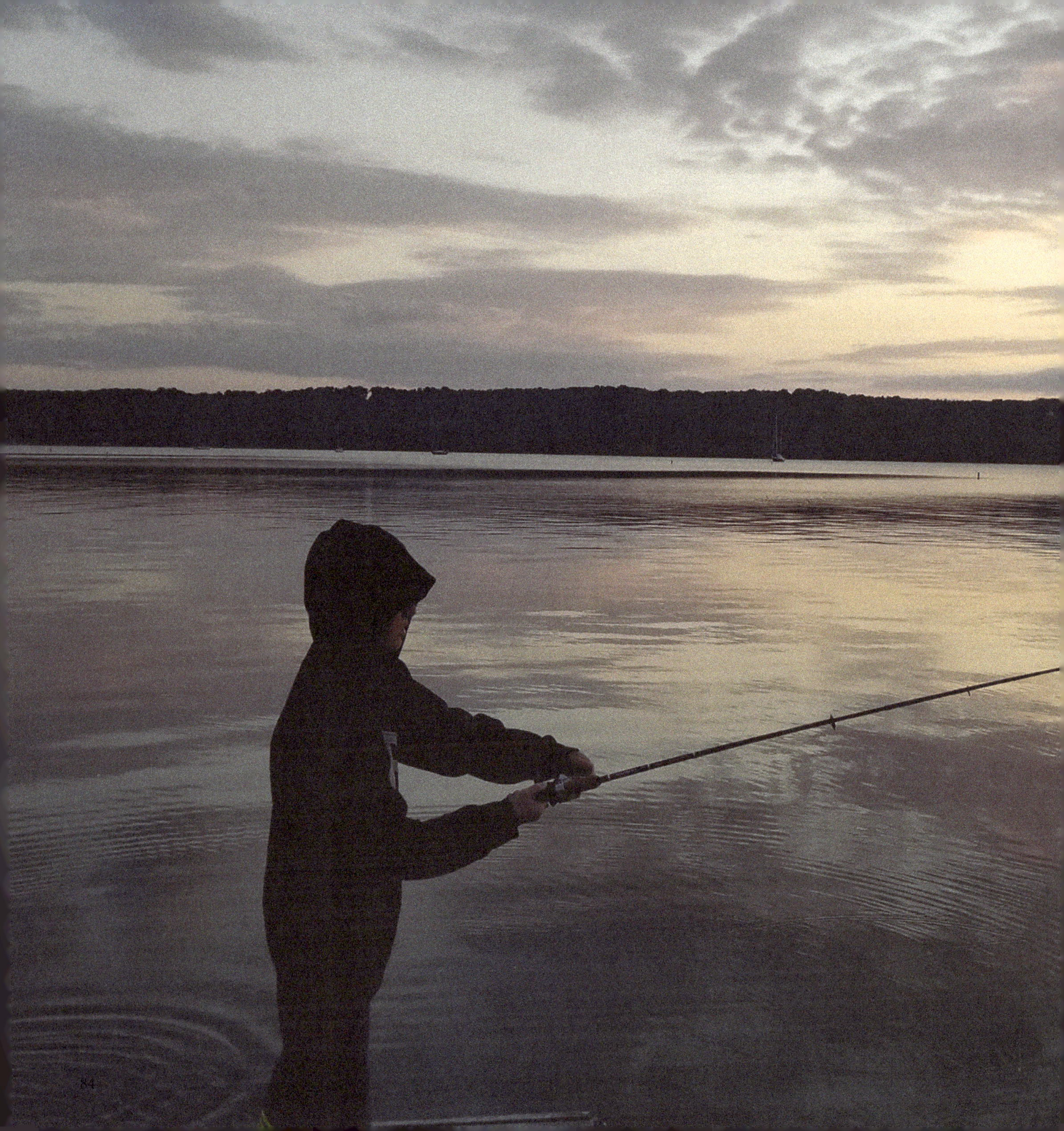

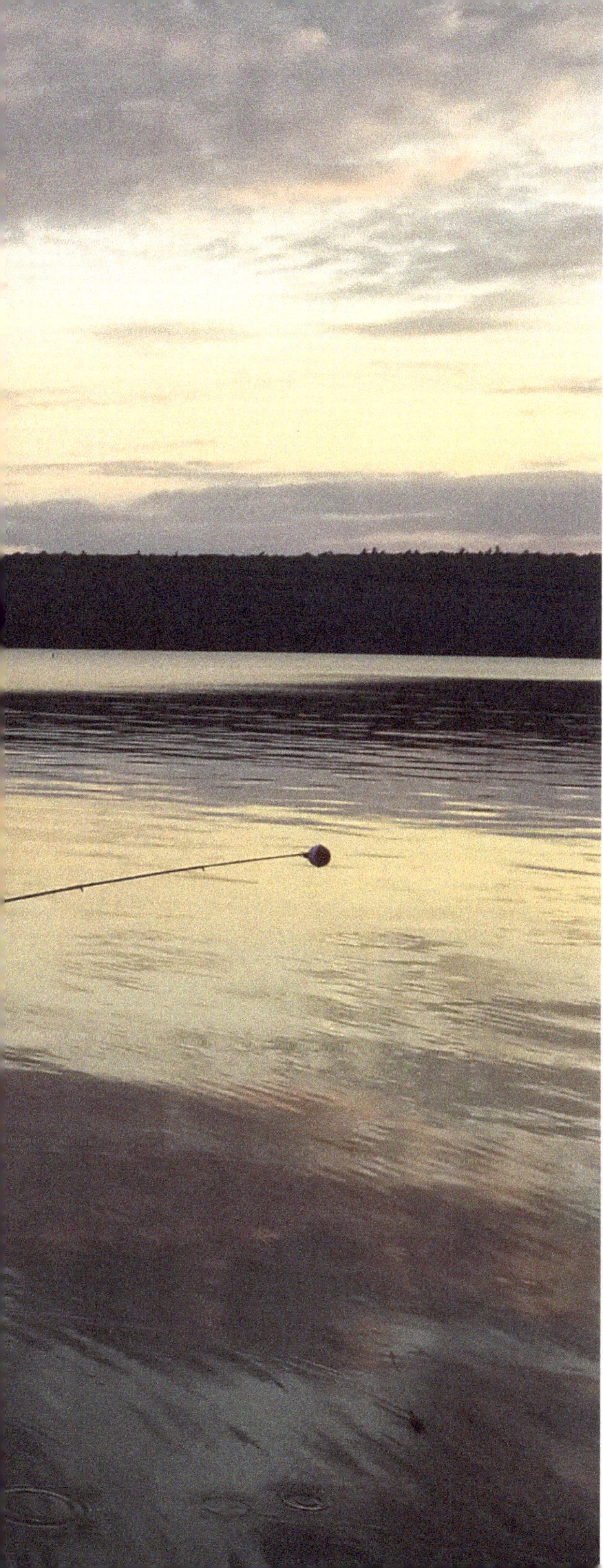

The Artist

A teen-something
angler
throws back his rod
casting long, gossamer
filament
into the languid bay.
Resplendent ripples
jig to and fro,
forming rock-a-bye
waves.

An Impressionistic
palette
of red brick gondola
bridges,
white furry
poodles,
chiseled-chin
boxers,
and gleeful children
created by fluid
strokes
of the angler's
paintbrush
skip
the water's surface.

Reflections
of
the atmosphere's
infinitesimal
boundaries
collaborate
in unison
with a motor boat's
wake
completing
a young Monet's
masterpiece.

Dog Speak

Cautious approaches.
Arc-like.
Side sniff.
Snouts touch.
Tushy sniff.
Downward dog stretches.
Gentle wags.

"You're okay,
I guess!"

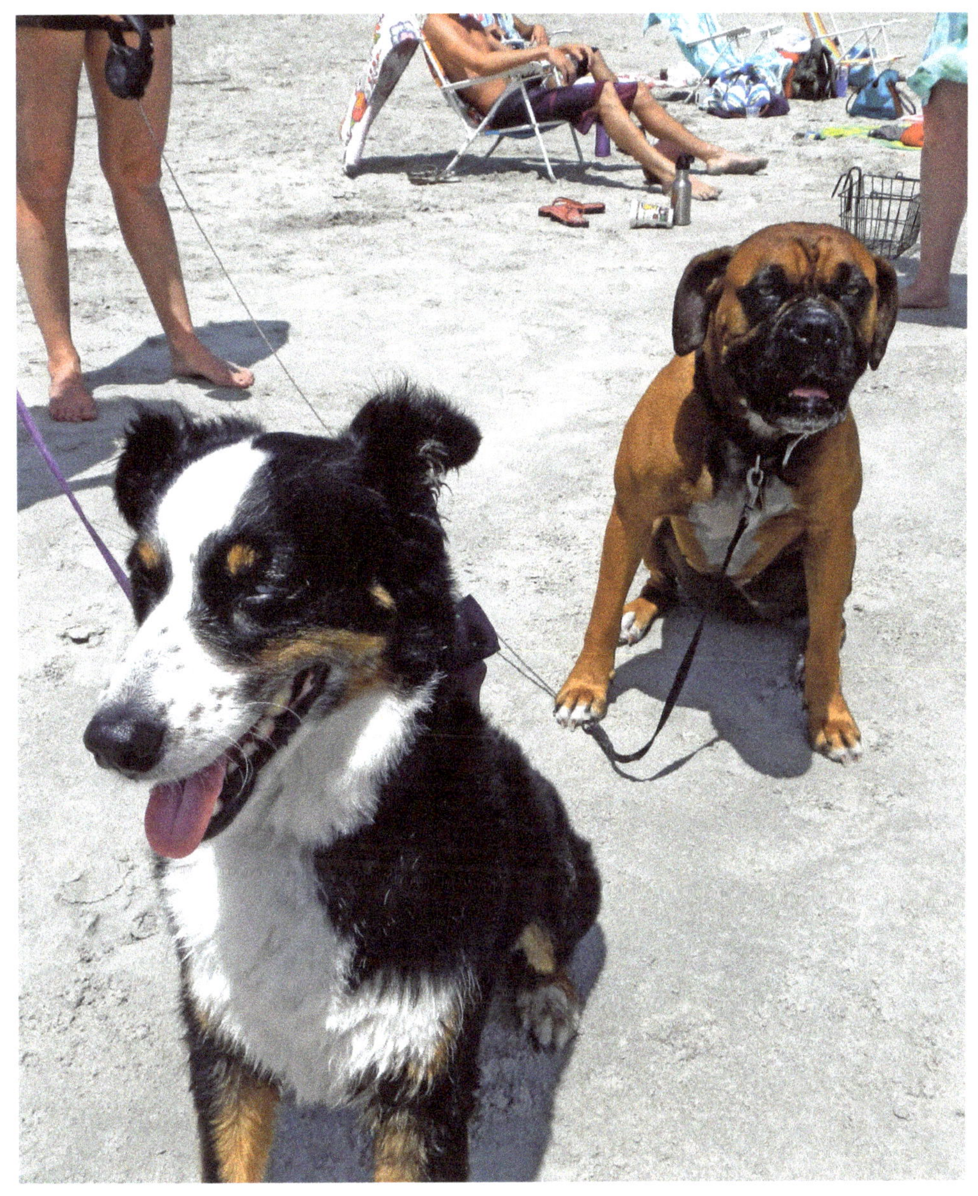

Someday, Dad

I'll meet you someday
at the Seven Mile Bridge
overlooking
a shimmering
sea
so aquamarine.

There'll be
thousands of fish
jumping
in every color
imaginable.

We'll fry up those fish
in your favorite
iron
skillet
and you'll
tell funny stories
to the Lord.

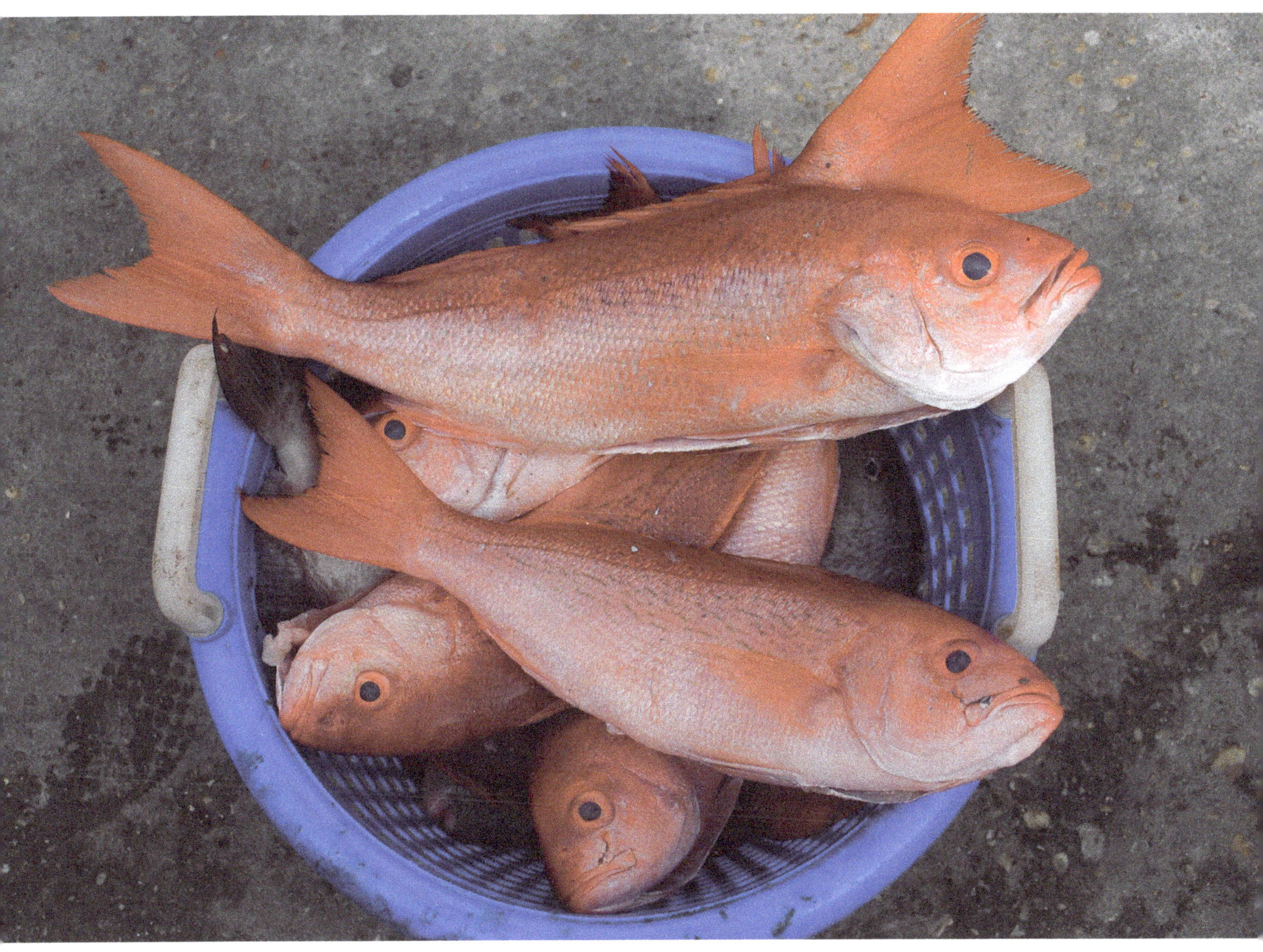

Black Cat

Black cat ponders
outside wonders –
crisp leaves whistling down
brisk autumn wind.

Mellifluous
Carolina chickadees
dance the jig
on wood rails,
foraging for seeds,
left by humans.

Black cat
rests comfortably
on the buttercream
cotton rug,
sun glistening,
warming coal black fur.

Black cat ponders life,
outside the big glass door,
tail swaying
to and fro
lemon eyes observing . . .
she secures a spot
near Red Dog.

The two
touch paw to paw
reposed
in the noonday sun.

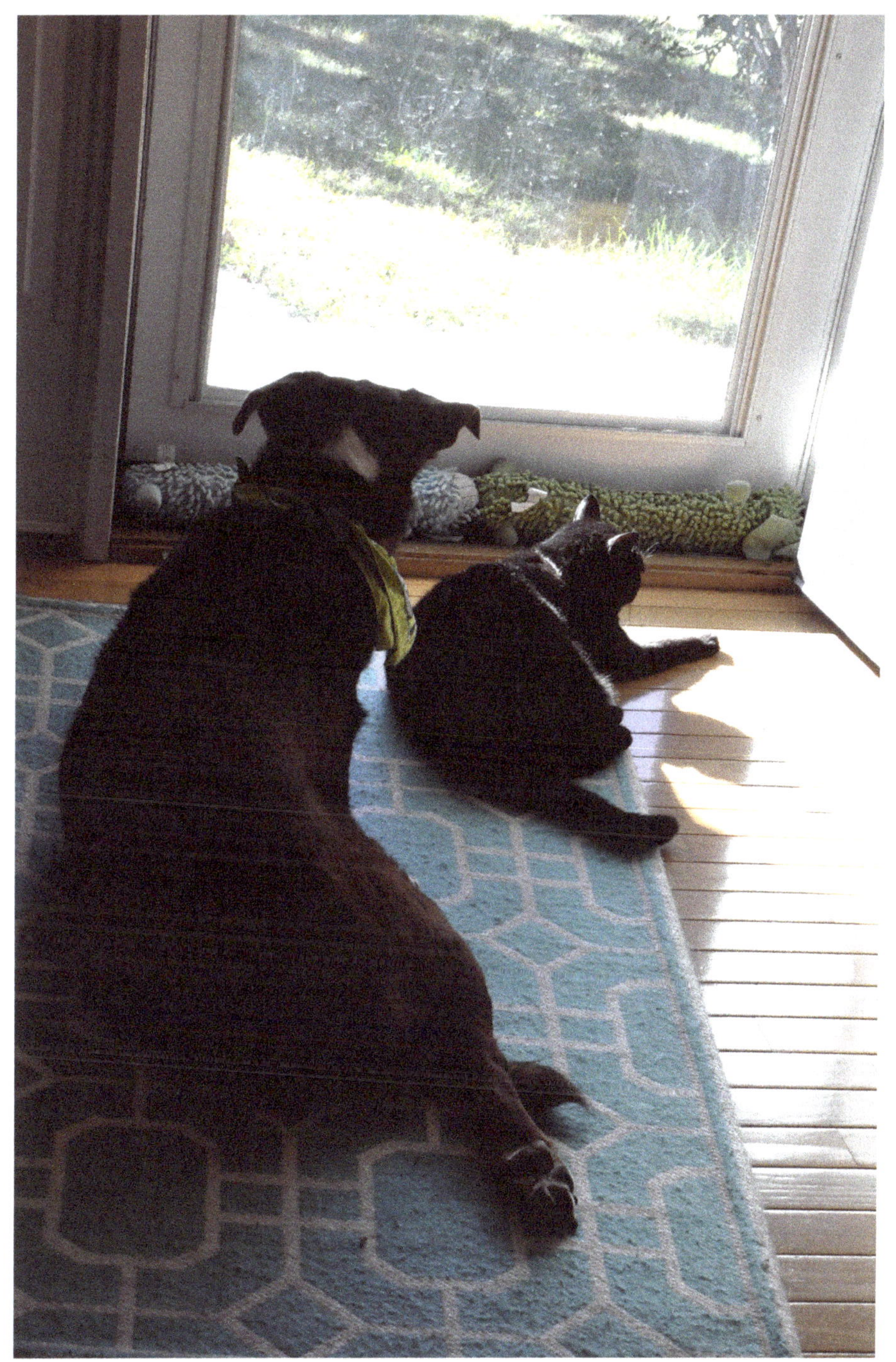

BEYOND

The beach beyond
the driftwood
remains
a mystery.

This place where
wind meets calm,
rough meets smooth,
arid meets wet . . .

A place of opposites
yet similarities
stir emotions
of contentment
and completeness
in my soul.

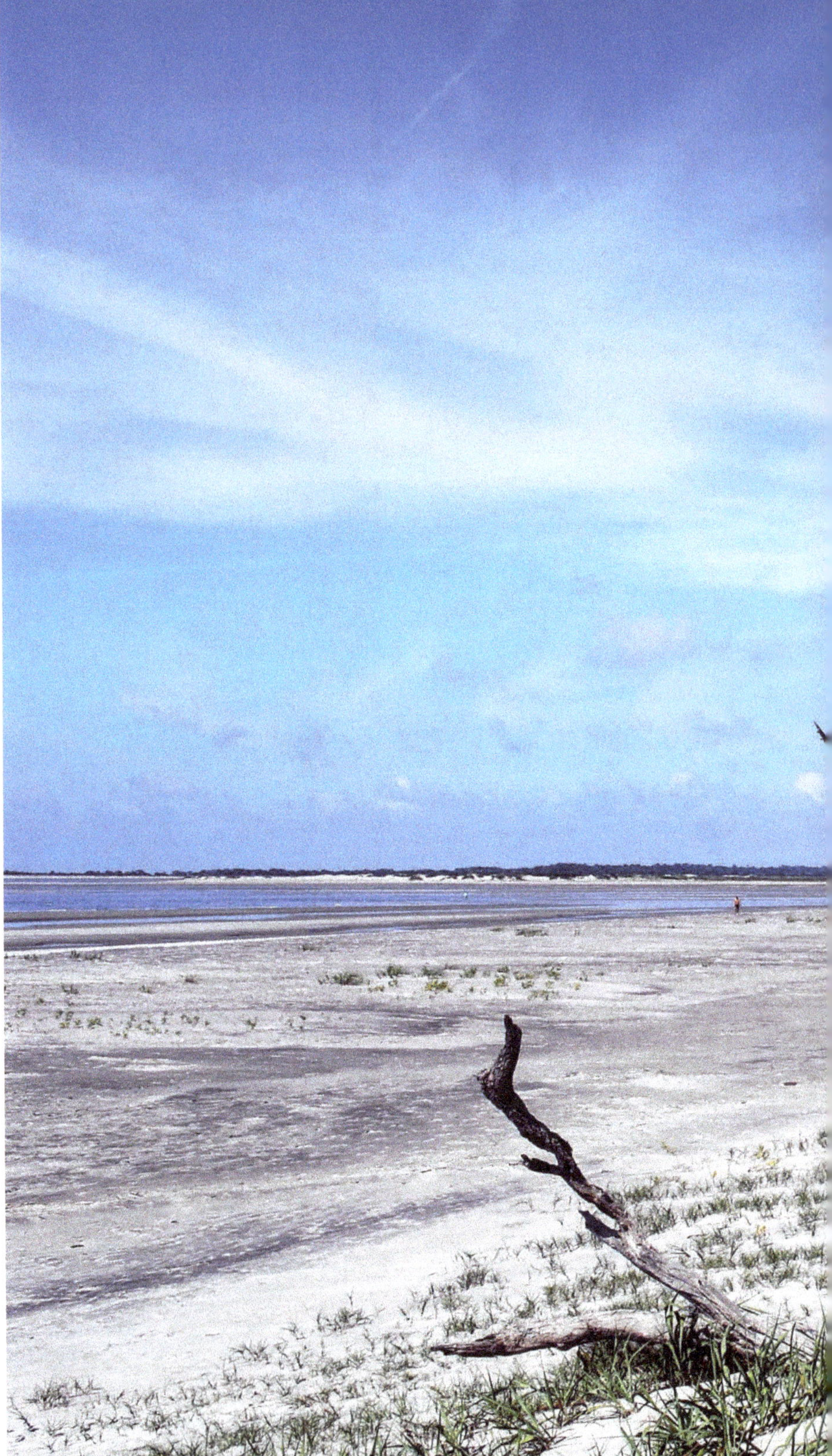

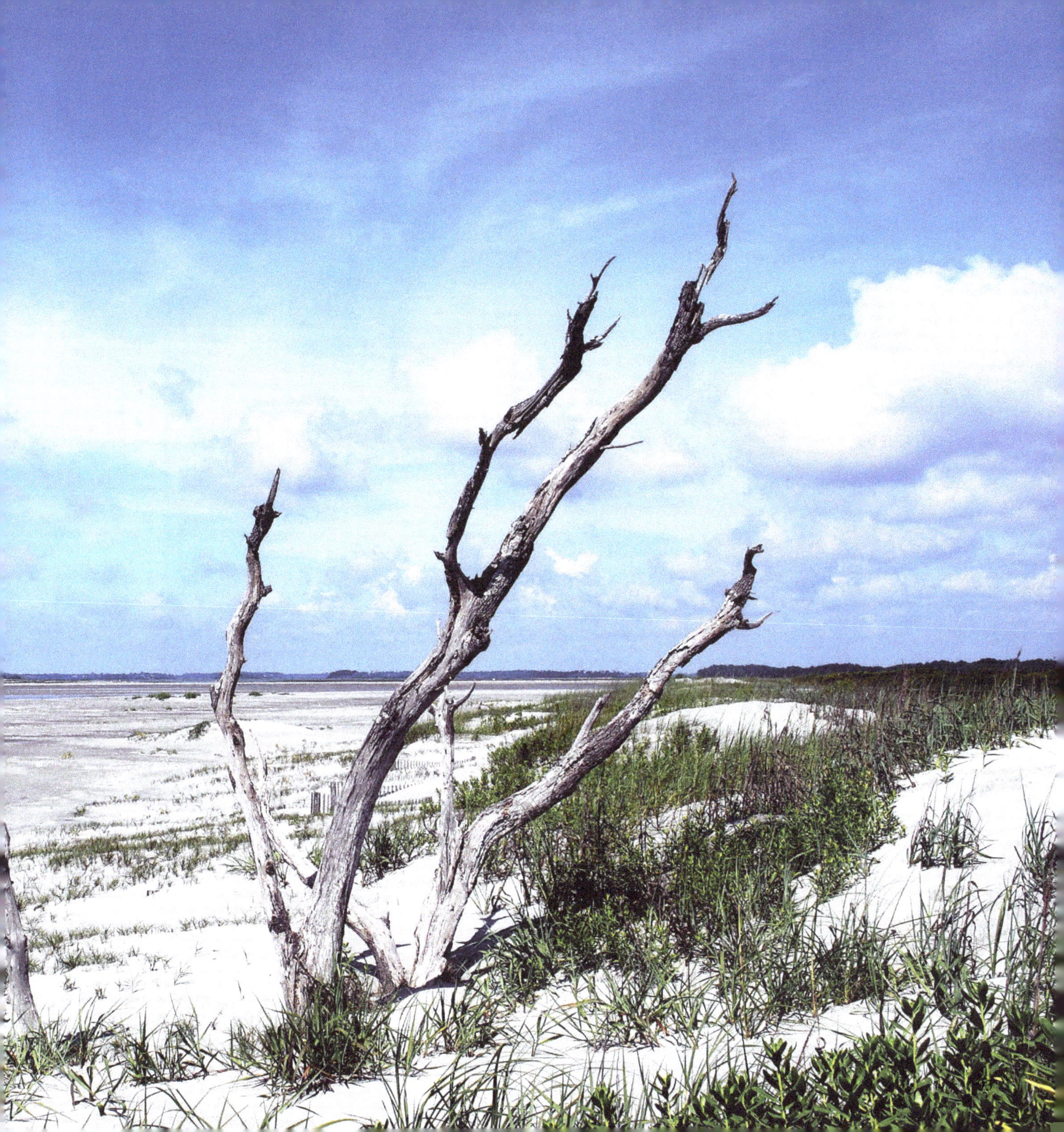

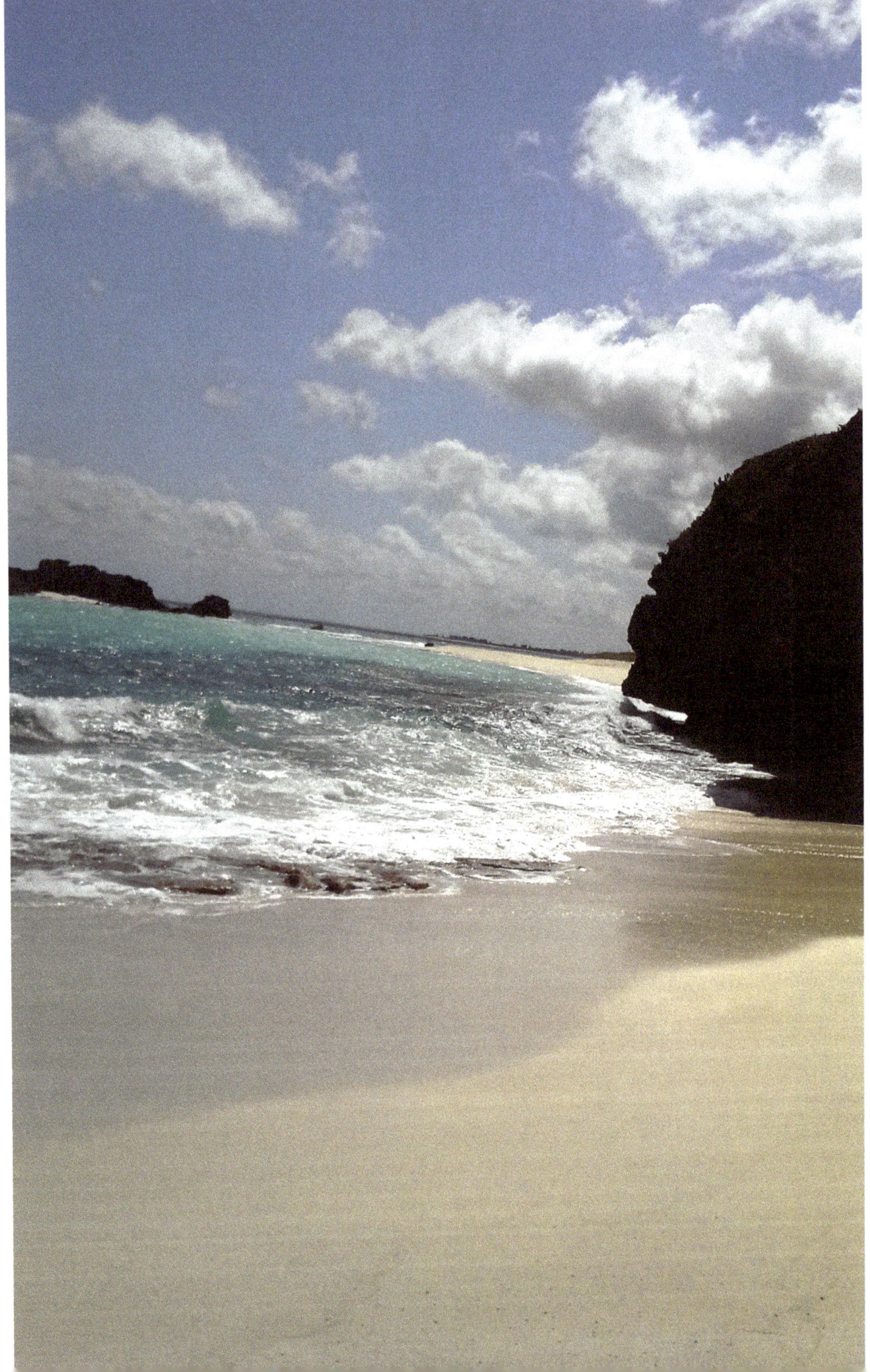

Visual Perceptions

The sunless sky
appears a misty haze
blurring
structures,
figures,
and natural
phenomenon,
beside the shore.

Sand
mimics the sea
as ripples
of white,
pewter
and celery green
intermingle
with shadows cast
by midday sun.

Clouds form
cotton candy pillows
tittering the atmosphere.

Seagulls
wistfully,
blissfully
soar above
the horizon.

My mind wanders
to easy days
and lazy nights
where campfires
linger
and glow,
conversations
flow
and time
takes
a much
needed
nap.

My Sea Shell Life

Once,
strong, unblemished
like an
Angel Wing.

Then,
sandy,
gritty,
broken,
discolored,
stepped on,
crushed underfoot.

Now,
A mature conch –
seasoned,
weathered,
but not worse
for the wear.

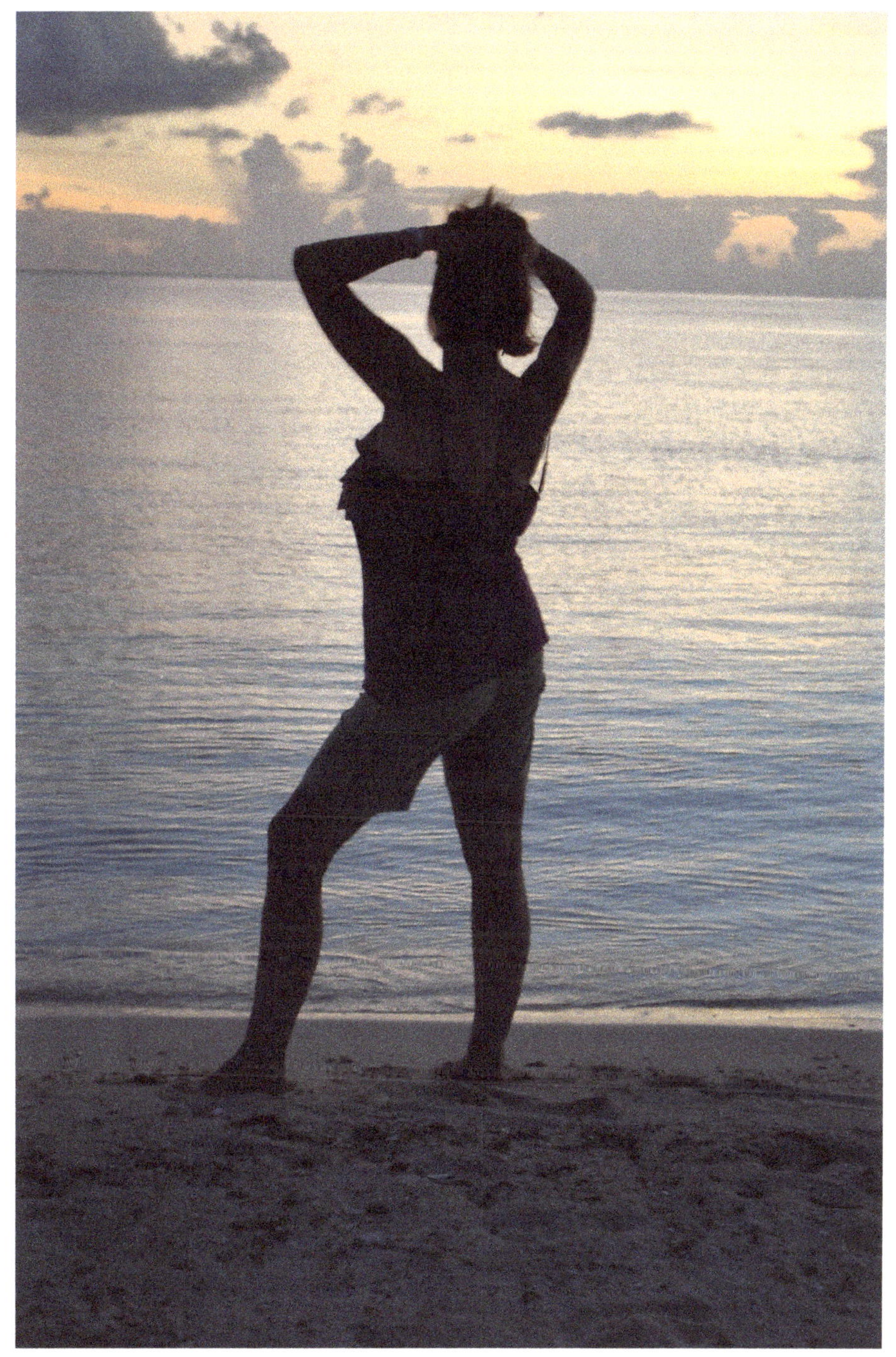

Midwest Sunset

Clouds fade
from cotton candy pinks,
charcoal greys,
and tangerine oranges
into shapes of dragons and horses,
while
oak trees
melt
into plowed fields,
brushy meadows
and golden ponds
in the company
of the
100-year-old
barn.

Nighttime awaits...

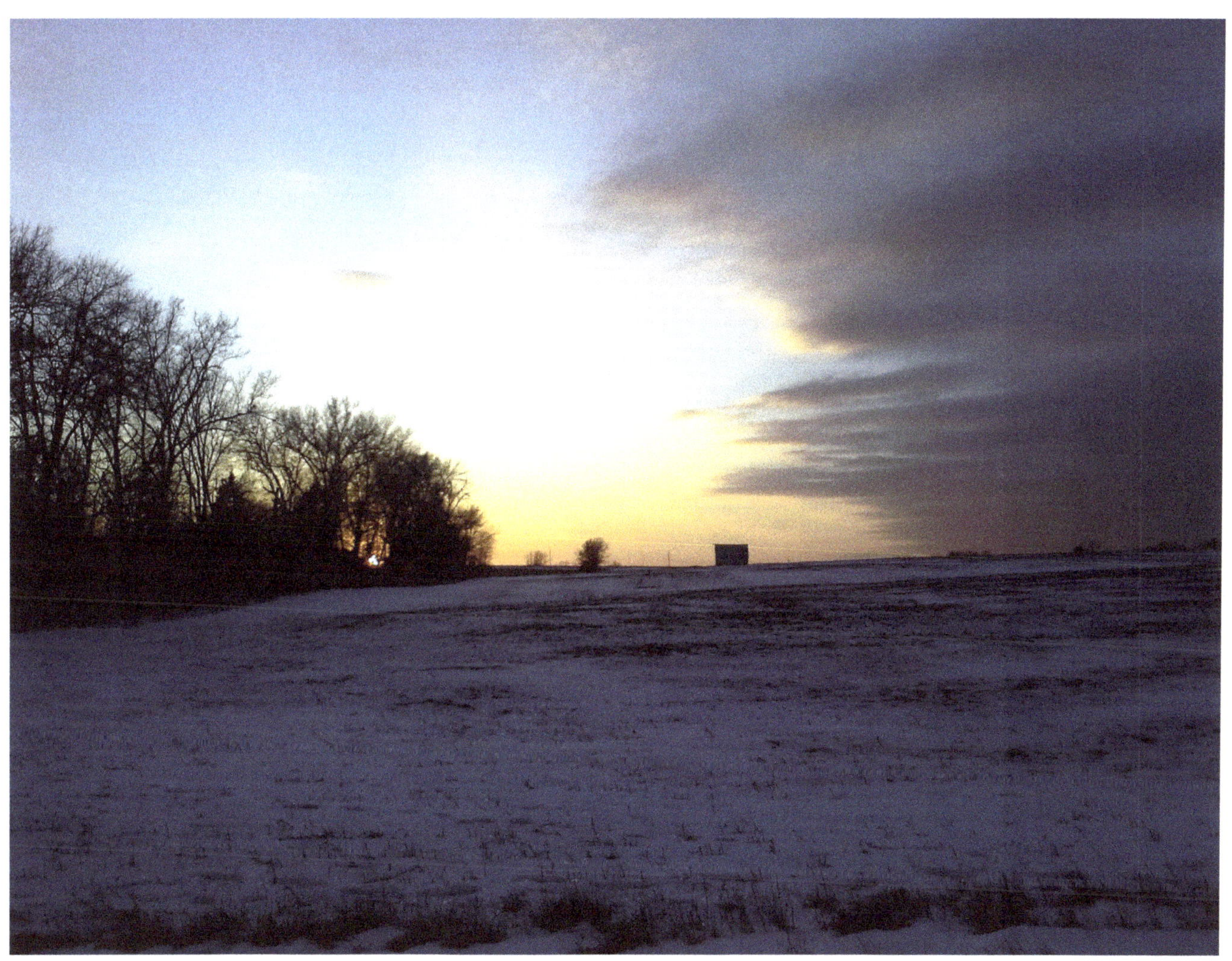

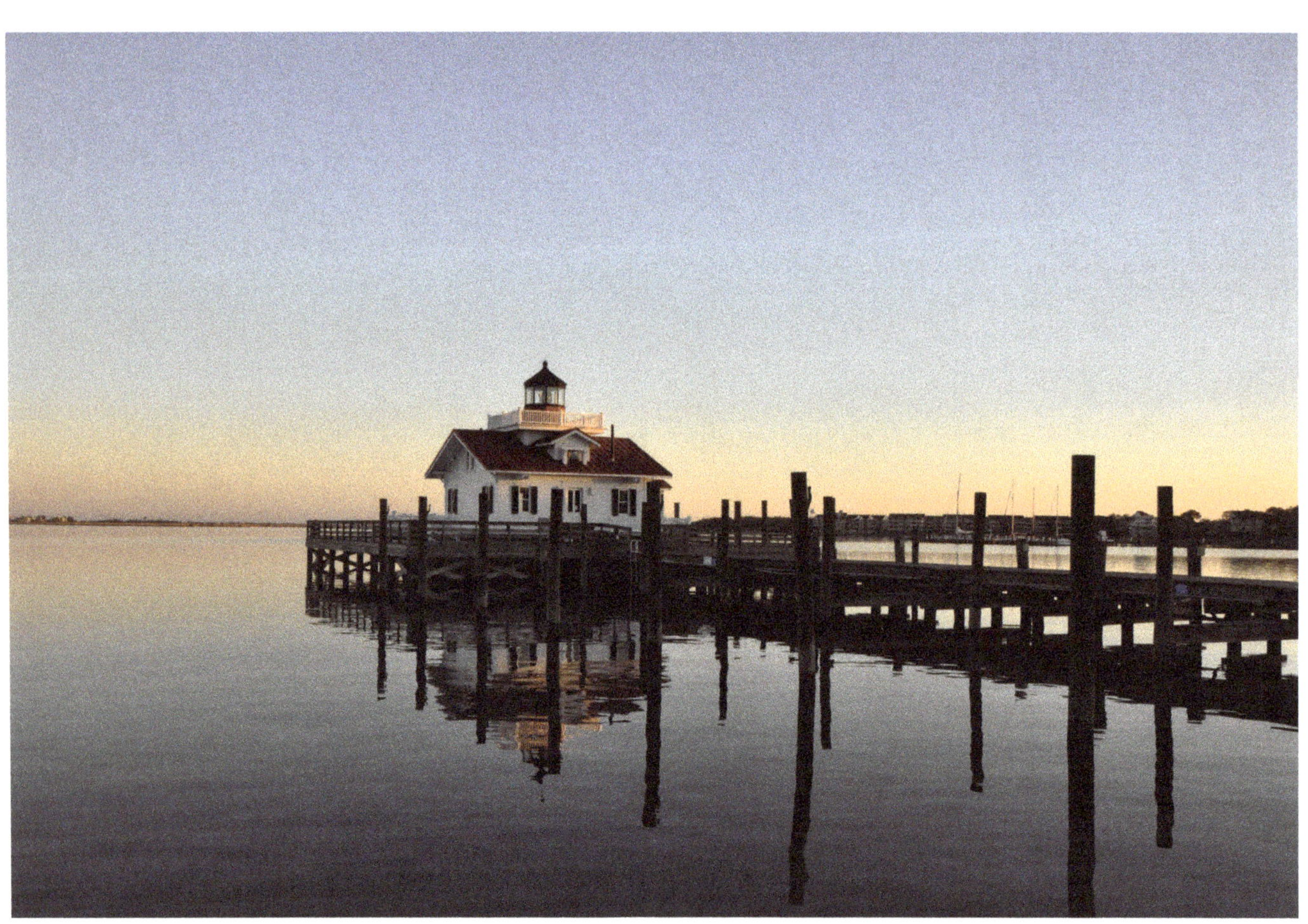

Star Gazing

The slow,
rocking motion
of the splintered dock
comforts,
as cool metal
nail heads
trace the vertebrae
in my spine.

The sky sprinkled
with the wisdom
of the universe –
Socrates, Pluto, Aristotle –
helps me escape
to the siren's song
in my soul.

The constellations
cast a glance my way.
I'm vulnerable
under the spell
of a Harvest Moon.

Acknowledgments

The author wishes to gratefully acknowledge the editors of the following publications in which these poems first appeared.

Well Versed 2018 Prose and Poetry: "Mondays in October," "Raspberry Point," and "Visual Perceptions"

Well Versed Literary Works 2017: "Living Water," "Red Dog's Observations," and "To The Seashore"

Well Versed Literary Works 2016: "Black Cat"

Well Versed Literary Works 2015: "Star Gazing"

Well Versed Literary Works 2014: "Ode to Sunset Beach"

Folly Beach Dances, 2014: "Beach Glass," "Dream Waltz," "Liquid Dancing," "The Ballet," and "The Drifter"

Folly Current Newspaper - Summer 2011: "Carolina Delight"

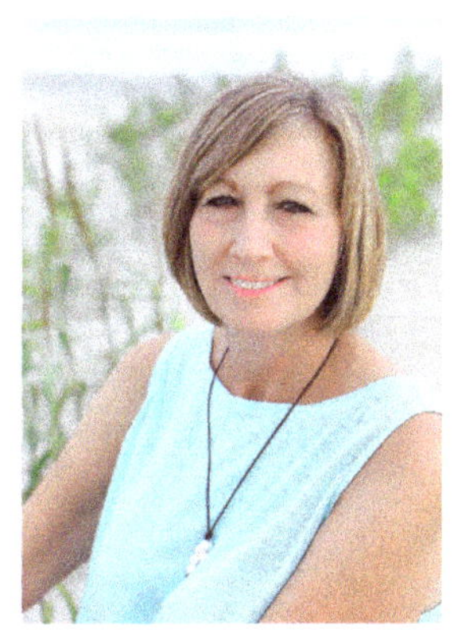

About Sheree K. Nielsen

A former circuit design engineer for a major telecom company, Sheree K. Nielsen believes that every picture tells a story, combining her love of photography and writing with colorful visual descriptions and healing messages found in her coffee table books, essay collections, children's books, and poems. She finds inspiration in the ocean and nature.

Sheree is author/photographer/poet of 2015 Da Vinci Eye Award Winner *Folly Beach Dances* (inspired by the sea and her lymphoma journey), Chanticleer Little Peeps First Place Category Winner and Montaigne Medal Finalist *Midnight the One-Eyed Cat* (a picture book; co-author), and Chanticleer Finalist *Ocean Rhythms Kindred Spirits — An Emerson-Inspired Essay Collection on Travel, Nature, Family and Pets.*

Her other works are well represented in *Southern Writers Magazine, AAA Southern and Midwest Traveler, Long Weekends, South and North Brunswick Magazine, Missouri Life*, among others.

When not writing, she is discovering new beaches and coffeehouses with her goofy dogs and patient husband. Four content cats complete her family.

Connect with Sheree at **www.shereenielsen.wordpress.com**.

CPSIA information can be obtained
at www.ICGtesting.com
Printed in the USA
LVHW071002240919
632102LV00018B/299/P

9 781947 067448